ONE EXCELLENT ADVENTURE

Seeing the West
with a Tent and a Truck

Beth Grigsby

For my husband, Jeff, and my children.

You have enriched my life.

Contents

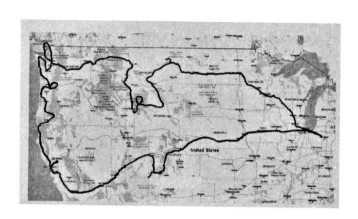

Our Adventure Route

ONE EXCELLENT ADVENTURE

Seeing the West

with a Tent and a Truck

Spring 1972

Everybody dreams. One of our dreams came true. Work was boring for my husband Jeff and me. We wanted some action in our life. One cold Minnesota night, we had an idea—do something unusual—and it involved travel.

"Wouldn't it be fun to see the west?" My husband Jeff said as he stretched his arms and the lumpy bed creaked.

"I have vacation hours I haven't used," I said.

"I'm talking months not days."

"That changes things. Possible, but it will take some doing. There's our stuff. What's behind all this?"

"I've never seen the west," he said, "and I want to. Primarily, I want the freedom that comes with having our own schedules, including when to set the alarm clock, picking our own routes, what to wear. Its corporate life is what I would like to forget for a while. Then there's the pressure to climb the ladder. I've had it. It's time to do something different."

When morning came, I made a list of everything we needed from food to towels. Our dream was taking shape.

"This list is invaluable," Jeff said. "Everything we need is here." As he scanned the list with his green eyes, he brushed his light brown hair out of his eyes so he could see better. Looking up from the list, he commented that it was not bad for two neophytes who haven't ever been camping.

"Now, about setting up the tent; we should give it a go before we leave. Watching us put up that tent will give someone a good laugh," he said with a twinkle in his eye. We tried anyway and had some moderate success.

Being a new bride, I went along with the idea of this trip. At first I was unsure. My skepticism quickly changed to enthusiasm once we started making plans. We could see what is out there. I was not tied to my job and could give it up, but as a new bride, I was willing even though we would live out of a tent, give up family and friends, and have a lot of togetherness.

We made our preparations and set out. Often, interesting people wandered into our camp at night. Most of the conversation was polite and light. Occasionally, the talk turned serious. We did enjoy meeting and talking with a variety of people.

Putting up that tent seemed like nothing compared to what we experienced with the motorcycle accident. It started like this.

"That guy is moving," Jeff said nervously from behind the wheel. From out of nowhere the young man swerved in front of us.

"It's rather dangerous. How fast do you think he is going?" I asked as we watched the young man and woman speed by us.

"I'm doing 65 and he's pulling away."

After taking care of everything with the motor-cycle accident, we left knowing there would be more adventures ahead. In front of us were bad storms, bears in our campground, naked dancers, an elegant restaurant in the most unlikely place, friends, the challenge of finally being home, and more. Each to be savored as part of One Excellent Adventure, seeing the west with a tent and a truck.

June 5

Our adventure began. My mother, Irene Brown Horton, opened her doors to us before we left. We used her house as home base, especially as we did some final preparations. She had us and our things. A lot of our possessions were sold and she kept the rest until we returned. We sure didn't know what the future would bring. But nothing was going to stop us. We had this gnawing inside us that had to be appeased, and we were convinced this road trip would bring satisfaction. Mom waved goodbye as we pulled the truck away from her curb. We were off to the west, not really having a destination in mind but thinking it would all work out.

Interstate 94 became our thoroughfare. The road took us away from our previous lives. The farther the better. We stopped at a roadside rest area for lunch at Bergen Lake, but its mass produced, concrete picnic tables stripped us of any outdoor feeling. Although traveling freeways is the fastest way to drive somewhere, it's harder to see and enjoy things along the way.

Like most, this day was uneventful. This was what I called a driving day. We made tracks. Usually, Jeff was in the driver's seat and I road shotgun. Occasionally, I relieved him from the monotony of the road. But this day was monumental for us because we had finally done it—dropped out of corporate life.

Our Home Away from Home

When evening came, we found ourselves in Buffalo River State Park, in the far western part of

Minnesota. We did all that driving and are still in the state, I thought, as we pulled into our camping spot that first night.

Although reading was almost new to us, at night we had to learn how to relax and to perfect our mosquito swatting skills. Mosquitos are annoying pests. They constantly reminded us that we had escaped from life as we knew it.

If we intended to sleep that night we had some tent work to do. Setting up our tent reminded me of those stereotypical moments when someone is trying to erect a tent and have no luck so the thing keeps falling down until the person either succeeds or completely fails. For us, it was almost comical. Two people with college educations should do better. Finally, the last stake went into the ground, and we stood back from the tent and admired our handiwork. Our home away from home.

As we prized our canvas abode, our faces flushed, we shouted, "Oh no," and our tent gracefully fell to the ground. That night, sitting at our campfire, flames tried to pierce the evening sky. I believe each twinkle was visible. Imagine far away stars and black holes. Each star in the clear sky had its unique dance. Then we met Tom, who was camped next to us and been out only two days on his way to Alaska.

"Hi neighbor, I'm Tom."

Throughout our adventure we seldom heard last names. Knowing them was unnecessary in this transient society. He leaped out of the bushes and invited himself over to our campfire where we learned he was from Ironwood, Michigan with Betty, his wife and two young grandchildren. He had only been out two days and had already broken down. We'd thought about breakdowns, which is one reason we bought a new truck with a good safety record.

Since his car broke down he needed a lift in the morning to the Ford dealership to pick it up. We were going through North Dakota anyway so dropping him off in Fargo was right on our way. After we said goodbye to Tom, we headed to Jamestown, North Dakota, where we discovered the "Heart of the North Dakota Prairie," Jamestown's way of saying, "The west starts here."

June 6

There it was. The 60-foot concrete buffalo so straight and tall near the town of Jamestown, North Dakota. After parking the truck, we got out, stretched, inhaled the fresh air, and hiked up to view the buffalo. I thought of cowboy hats, grungy boots, jeans, big belt buckles, rodeos, ropes, horses, saddles and, of course, cattle. I let my imagination do its thing and conjured up whatever the words west and freedom meant. Here we were, getting a taste of sights, sounds, and smells of things to come. It was exhilarating, truly different from our day-in-day-out jobs.

Not far from the buffalo, tourists could view a pioneer village though we found it boring. The only thing that saved us was spending 45 minutes talking with a Native American woman who told us things such as powwows are gatherings of tribes and communities to sing, dance, canoe, and socialize.

"The village is fun," she said, "but I have a better time with my friends."

She and her friends went through Ely, Minnesota before their canoe trip began.

Jeff looked at me while he told her that we knew about Ely because Minnesota was our home. It's a small town, a starting point for many as they paddle the Boundary Waters Canoe Area (BWCA) or just the "Boundary Waters" as many refer to nature at its best. It attracts those willing to trade convenience for pristine lakes, tall pines and bird songs.

The woman was of medium height, young, with long, flowing black hair and high cheekbones. She was dressed in traditional garb: a floor-length leather dress with a fringed yoke and hem. Tiny white beads outlined the yoke and three quarter length sleeves. Black and red beads were fashioned into a long necklace with matching pierced earrings. The tourists loved seeing her. This was one of the few encounters with a Native American they would ever have, and they enjoyed seeing and meeting her.

We left Jamestown for the nearby Fort Abraham Lincoln National Park in North Dakota, situated near the Missouri River and high above great expanses of prairie grasses, truly something to experience not just see. Fort Lincoln is an interesting place for history buffs and those into anything Native American. In addition to earth mound houses, Fort Lincoln garrisoned Lt. Col. George A. Custer. He and his troops left from there to meet the Sioux in the Little Big Horn battle.

We toured the recreated areas of the park, including Custer's home, and drove over to the earth lodges. At one time this location was a fully functioning village with many earth lodges, families, possessions, animals and outlying fields of crops needed to sustain them.

The earth lodges are domed structures some being about 60 feet in diameter, others about 90 feet, and completely covered with earth. The bigger ones are ceremonial places rather than individual homes. Smoke from the center of the earth lodge is vented through a hole in the center of the roof. (For more information on earth lodges go to "earth lodges" on your computer or tablet browser.)

The sun was setting so it was time to hustle to our campsite for the night. We camped in the western part of North Dakota. Medora and Theodore Roosevelt Park were our stop for the night.

"Doing this every night is a real pain," Jeff uttered as he removed his lips from the air mattress's nozzle and sucked in some fresh air. I have a better idea. Why don't we just keep them inflated since everything is thrown in the back anyway?"

"Sounds great, a good idea," I said. My turn came and I puckered up, wrapped my lips around the nozzle, and blew.

Theodore Roosevelt Park

We came to this park not knowing its majestic presence or stunning landscape, a hidden gem tucked away by dust and distance. Tomorrow we will look around.

June 7

There it was. We finally reached our destination—Prairie Dog Town in Theodore Roosevelt Park. Enough of spindly pine trees, a muddy river winding through a path to an ocean, and short grass and tall weeds never tasting sickness and death via chemicals. We had arrived.

We found a place to park the truck. No signs to interpret. No people to negotiate with regarding taking the spot. No meters to plug. We just pulled off the dirt road, put the truck in park, and hiked to see what we could.

From where we were, across an area of about 500 x 500 feet of sandy soil, we saw more little golden brown prairie dogs and their habitat than anyone could have counted. They look like squirrels, only slightly bigger and are just as mean. Some stood erect, but on their back legs, acting like sentries always watching for predators. Others were content in their burrows.

They often peeked their heads out of the holes they found to check the landscape. Seeing the prairie dogs reminded me of the game played by kids in which every time a prairie dog stuck out its head, it was struck by a mallet. Whenever a prairie dog popped his head out of a burrow it just looked around, and back he went.

The next thing we knew we were back at the truck talking to a middle-aged couple who had pulled up behind us. Our conversation started with the usual formalities.

"Where are you going?" we asked.

"Oregon."

They seemed friendly enough. I have always evaluated people because there are a lot of weirdos around, and I am rather protective. But this couple seemed normal. The talking continued:

"Where are you folks from?" Jeff quietly asked the couple.

"Niggertown, Baltimore," the man bellowed.

We were so embarrassed and looked around to see if there were some who might have heard him. Fortunately, there were not but what a thing to say! His comment threw us totally off-base so we excused ourselves and left.

That night we attributed his hate language to ignorance—the only way we could understand and interpret what happened during our chat with that fellow. Thoughts of the day invaded our sleeping bags and we both tossed and turned. Sleep finally came and gushed over our canvas walls in rhythm with the rain, and tomorrow would still be another day.

June 8

This morning, we drove to a place called Buck Hill. Not knowing what to expect, we were pleasantly surprised. Beneath this high, stone overlook we spied a herd of shaggy buffalos as well as a herd of wild horses. Both groups munched on what we thought was sweet grass from the nearby flow of the Little Missouri River. Then a big, white-tailed deer emerged from the fragrant bushes. We were stunned. Apparently, he was not and if he smelled us he chose to show himself.

Buck Hill has a view impossible to describe. It is so stunning it left lasting memories. That afternoon, and even though there was more to do and see, we focused on the little town of Medora, North Dakota. In this town of just over a hundred people, some don't mind dirt pretending there is asphalt on their streets or where hitching posts and wooden walkways are transformed into concrete. Later, we came barreling around a corner and once the dust from the street settled saw a large, stately, two-story house.

Our mouths fell in unison when we spotted the blue, Chateau de More mansion, which we soon learned once belonged to the Marquis More. It seemed highly out of place among the scrubby trees, dirt everywhere, and rugged people. Far too elegant for western North Dakota. Of course, it started to rain.

We got to know rain intimately because it followed us, it seemed like forever. Occasionally, it got the best of us. On those days, we stayed in cheap motels, the kind with paper-thin walls and sticky carpeting. We showered but we also went against the rules and hauled in our camp stove and cooked. Rules didn't seem to matter much out here.

June 9

Theodore Roosevelt Park is magnificent, and it's easy to see why Teddy liked it here. But, our gear is packed so it is time to say goodbye and see what's in store for us in Montana. When we crossed the line, I envisioned handsome cowboys, big ranches, and fat cattle. What I saw were regular people, rundown ranches, and thin cattle trying to find sustenance.

Montana is truly Big Sky country with two distinct regions: the east and the west. We were definitely in the eastern, less mountainous, part. On our way we stopped at a hole in the wall diner for lunch in the little town of Wolf Point. The diner had a creaky wooden floor and falling-off-the-walls wallpaper. Old oak booths with high backs lined one side, a matched row on the other. A lot of tables were scattered throughout the middle. A black fly buzzed inside the glass-tiered pie stand. Patrons enjoyed morning coffee on comfortable, round, swivel stools situated below the gray Formica counter tops. Customers tried to recognize faces in photographs hung on the walls, but it was time to move on. In the truck we studied the map, found a campground just outside of Wolf Point, and away we went.

We felt we were the only ones to experience the feeling of being on the top of the world and seeing this big, blue sky. No one was in view and we felt the change in elevation due to Montana being high, and our bodies reacted when just breathing became more difficult. Suddenly, we were light-headed and our limbs went limp. We needed gas, stopped at the old-fashioned service station, and told some local folks about our condition. They nodded when someone said "altitude sickness," and "It'll pass." We were only about 4,000 feet, but it did not matter to our bodies. Since we now had a diagnosis, prognosis, and the condition had a name, we felt better immediately. It was back to the comfortable ride of the truck and the next thing on our agenda—getting a campsite and settling in for the night.

We read the map carefully. It showed a campground symbol just outside Wolf Point. When we got there, we were surprised to find a pasture. We cautiously inched the truck along the narrow path. On either side of us were brown and white-faced cattle, occasionally a black one in the mix, as well as tall weeds, a little grass, and hundreds of cow pies.

"It's on the map so it's out here somewhere." Jeff's voice crept up as he felt the frustration.

"Surely, it's got to be here," I agreed.

But, no campground.

"I don't know." Now Jeff lost confidence in find-ing a spot.

I, too, wanted to pitch our tent for the night but this place did not look promising. By now, of course, it was raining. We gave the rain a worried look and continued. Peering about and stretching out our necks, we kept hoping to see someone or something that reminded us of a campground.

"Looks like it's not going to let up," Jeff said. "Plus I cannot find the campground, if there is really one." Still not giving up, he kept looking around. He finally gave up, and we drove to little Jordan, Montana, and a motel for the night.

June 10

After having breakfast in the room, courtesy of our big, green cooler which contained everything we needed, including a little toaster, we headed out to find the ranch of our distant relatives, Walter and Lucille, near Lewistown. We had a vague route identified although we were unsure how to actually find the place. But, Montana had other plans for us.

Naturally, rain was involved. The rain fell down. Before long it got bad. Now the road became a big mud hole. When we came to the worst part we could barely see. Our windshield wipers tried to keep up, but could not. Traffic was sliding every which way. Finally, the rain subsided, and we were relieved but what an experience.

Through some miracle, we found the ranch and Walter and Lucille. We ventured down their nearly half mile, bumpy driveway to a warm greeting from them both. Then, after introductions and the customary comments and questions, Walter showed us around.

"We got 1300 acres and run about one hundred cattle," Walter said, adjusting his worn cowboy hat, making him look more grizzled. He wore old jeans and a plaid shirt. He dressed like a rancher.

"Here's our barn and a couple horses and over there's the house, Lucille got it fixed up real good. I was raised in that house, three of my own grew up there." Walter fondly looked toward the simple structure with its clapboard siding and peeling paint.

"Lucille's worked hard on the inside, now it's bright and cheery," he added.

We looked around and saw everything a ranch would have. Back home we would call it a farm with different architecture but similar machinery. Now, it was on to Lucille and the house.

She waited for us at the kitchen door. She wore blue jeans, and her dark, silver-streaked hair was in a knot at the back of her head. Her face strained, she looked like she had already worked hard that day.

"We are sure glad you're here," she said as she welcomed us into their home. "You're staying for supper, aren't you?" The day had been long and we were exhausted. Too much rain and too many muddy roads. We were glad to have found the ranch. Although we had not intended to be there at mealtime, a two-hour traffic delay and the constant downpour changed our plans, and there we were.

Lucille showed us the sparse inside. In the bright kitchen was a well-worn table surrounded by several mismatched chairs. Lucille told us the attic was filled with beds all covered with quilts. The tour complete, it was time to eat.

We sat around the rectangular table on the wood chairs. Walter began to talk and had many tales to tell. For instance, the time, during a blizzard, he drove his son on a tractor down the long, bumpy driveway so his son could catch the school bus. He also talked about having no speed limit in Montana but in one in Wyoming where it was 75.

He was not happy about even 75. At that that point, I saw Walter as a grizzled rancher, not afraid of anything. He'd seen it all.

When it was Lucille's turn, she talked about taking hunters "down to the coolie" (a remote area having water nearby)." She seemed to have good luck and I sensed a rivalry between her and Walter. But, we moved on to talk about family, and what it was like to raise children out there.

The western sun was low in the sky and it was time to go. The old clock on the wall chimed seven o'clock and we had to find a campsite in this terrible weather. I had to comment on supper, because it was so good. Lucille told me everything on the table, all meat, potatoes, vegetables, homemade bread including the butter and even the dessert came from the ranch. The supper was something I will never forget. Our attention turned to what was happening outside.

The rain came down in sheets, lightening streaked across the sky, revealing big thunderheads above. The winds toppled trees near us and the temperature dropped. We had to go out in this storm and set up our tent somewhere plus haul our gear, and then try to sleep. Unbelievable, but we would if we had to. Luckily, Lucille glanced out the window and asked us to stay. We looked at each other, and accepted. It looked pretty bad out there.

She guided us through their bedroom to a ladder suspended from the wall of the hole in the ceiling. After scaling the entrance to the attic, we found a large room filled with beds waiting to be filled. One look around and surprise overtook us. We snuggled under a warm quilt and settled in for the night, content to be there, out of the horrible weather.

June 11

Today was a driving day after leaving Walter and Lucille's ranch. We headed toward Billings. Near Billings is a small area called Huntley. We stopped in Huntley for lunch, nestled up to the bar at Bernie's Bar and Grill where you could order either a hamburger or a hamburger and ate the best hamburger, wrapped in a fresh Kaiser bun. The hamburger came innocently on a small, paper plate. It was free from all trappings--no lettuce, tomatoes or onions. No pickles or, God forgive us, special sauce. Just a pure greasy hamburger. If someone wanted cheese, it was allowed; otherwise, it was completely meat. We devoured our hamburgers, wiped our faces, and left.

As the day progressed, we drove outside Billings to a place called Pompey's Pillar. Here William Clark, of the Lewis and Clark expedition, autographed and dated a rock. There were no reenactors, no visitor center so, of course, we were disappointed. What was there beneath the overgrown grass was a smooth rock that looked more like a boulder, but it was still just a rock. We noted the rock and left.

From the rock, we drove to Custer National Park. The famous battlefield area of the Little Big Horn Mountains was filled with ghosts. Everywhere we looked, we saw Custer and his troops of the 7th Calvary meet the Sioux Indians, both sides fighting to their deaths. Where people dropped, the park service had erected a small memorial commemorating each person. The battlefield is covered with these slate markers. This is certainly a sobering place. Easy to forgive the lack of facilities.

After sightseeing all day we were ready to hang it up. Our final stop for the day was a Kampground of America (KOA) in Sheridan, Wyoming. We often stayed at KOAs. They are the McDonalds of campgrounds. We were assured of consistency. The certain sameness found in McDonalds was found at KOA, so we knew what to expect. KOAs were mostly reliable places with clean spaces including the bathrooms. For the most part, visitors had easy registrations, reasonable rates, adequate spaces, warm showers, a convenient market, and good locations, all designed for the traveler. KOAs were functional, an easy in, easy out. What they lacked in ambiance they made up for in services. After a day on the road, KOAs were good places to rest our weary selves.

June 12

What a day! It started in Sheridan, Wyoming and ended in Wapiti Valley, Wyoming about 30 miles east of Yellowstone National Park. The day included beautiful scenery, parched land, museums, and a severe motorcycle accident.

Our speedometer registered about 65, and the road curved. Out of nowhere a black motorcycle passed us. The driver and his female passenger, who held him tightly around the waist, wore no helmets. By now, we were in beautiful Ten Sleep Canyon, another scenic area in Wyoming. The next thing we knew we were being flagged down by a teenaged girl. She turned out to be the daughter of the man who saw the accident. Apparently, he needed help. She waved us down but was also on her way to find a phone to call an ambulance. We saw the crumpled motorcycle alongside the road and immediately left the truck and jumped through a barbed-wire fence to get to the victim and to the man who was either hit or helping. We found them. They were in the cold creek in the water. Gary and Jillian were the victims and on the motorcycle when the accident occurred. She sat on the creek bank crying and calling out for Gary. Other than a few bruises and a lot of road rash Jillian seemed un- hurt. At least she was dry. The bystander man held Gary's head by the hair to keep him from drowning.

"What do you want us to do?" Jeff shouted to the Good Samaritan. We were frantic now.

"Hold his head up and out of the water until the ambulance comes," barked the man, so we got into the water and saw what a mess this guy was. We were convinced he'd broken both arms and both legs and damaged who knows what else. All I could do was comfort Gary until help came. Finally, we heard a siren in this remote part of the country.

"It won't be long now, they're coming," I said, stroking Gary's head and I thought we heard voices, but there were none, only hope that some- one would come and help. Besides all Gary's phys- ical woes, understanding him was easy, especially surprising. "You hold him underneath," said Jeff, "and we'll move him to the creek bank, out of this water." Gary screamed and begged for relief from the retching pain imprinted all over his face. We struggled to move Gary to the side rather than up the sandy bank; he was in too much pain to do more.

After what seemed like hours, the ambulance arrived. Out came two men, who ran to the back of a red and white, late model Chevy Suburban with double doors on the rear. They opened a door and pulled out a gurney. The workers wore cowboy hats and well-worn boots along with plaid shirts and blue jeans. They had certainly picked up many broken people before so there was hope underneath the victims' pain. The girl pointed them toward her father and the victim and off they ran.

Gary was consumed with pain but help had arrived. The EMT's, Jeff and I got him up the bank to the ambulance. We opened the back doors and tried to put Gary in. His legs hung at 90-degree angles to the sides of the back doors. We rearranged him and tried again. Gary screamed more and cussed in pain. When he was inside, the workers propped his legs up for the ride. The unhurt girl crawled into the ambulance and off they raced. We stayed a few more minutes and then, still breathing hard, went on our way.

We drove through Worland, a small town, and past the hospital where, we thought, Gary was being treated. We wondered about him. He was, in all sense of the words, lucky to be alive. Had the Good Samaritan not have been driving behind Gary and not witnessed the accident, Gary could have drowned in the creek. All this time, Jillian seemed distant. Perhaps she was in shock over what happened. That she had no major injuries was a miracle. She was concerned about Gary. Even though we already had had quite a time with the accident, now we were on our way to return to the town of Buffalo, here in Wyoming.

We were on the back roads and saw some of the most beautiful scenery imaginable. The majestic Little Big Horn Mountains had snow-caps even in June, and the valleys were filled with short wildflowers, some purple others pink, then there were the white ones and the yellow ones and an occasional orange one, all draped in the green of foliage. A path got us to the bottom of a valley. The gravel crunched under our footsteps. A sign reminded us that on either side there was native tundra that had taken hundreds of years to mature so we looked but stayed on the path. This was like a picture book of pretty scenes from nature. But for us, it was not just a photograph. What an experience! And it helped soothe the stress of the accident.

As we went to Buffalo, we felt like we were high in the sky. Wyoming is dry here. We were winded. But, the view was worth any discomfort. There was beauty as far as our eyes could see. The tree line marked true desolation above. Nothing grew up there. Aprons of rock surrounded the peaks. A lot of people hiked on one part so we could see ant-like trails above us leading to the top of a mountain. But we had to get going.

We got to Buffalo without ever seeing a real buffalo. But right outside the city hall stood a bronze statue of a buffalo. The statue was either full-size or bigger and welcomed folks. We enjoyed the small town by walking around and seeing Main Street, the shops and the other businesses. As we wandered the town, we came across a museum. Even better, admission was free. The James Getchall Memorial Museum contained artifacts from the old west. There were guns, paintings and paraphernalia from the past, including a beat-up wagon. We were definitely in the real west. After touring Buffalo and seeing the museum, it was time to go. We left knowing the day was not over.

Before we could close the day, we had a scenic ride that turned out better than some. The drive in the mountains was both beautiful and treacherous. The roads were often gravel and always curved and narrow. Many followed old animal paths; some were carved out of the mountain side. People stretched and took in views of adjacent mountains that shone in the snow. We went over Powder River Pass, elevation 9,666, the highest pass Jeff had ever been through.

"Going through a pass is no big deal," Jeff said. "It's just a sign."

"Well, what did you expect?" I knew going over the pass was simple.

"I guess a little fanfare and some changes to the arid land."

A sign indicated the pass name and elevation. We pulled over on a roadside turnout where I got out and snapped a picture of Jeff standing straight and tall right next to the sign. Even at this turnout the wild greenery was brown and parched.

From the pass, we drove down the mountain, keeping our eye on the close edge the entire way to Meadow Lark Lake. Here, we filled our water jug right from the lake. Cold mountain water from a lake so clear made a person anticipate the reward: thirst quenching and refreshing water. People can often only read about places like this. We were lucky.

That night we camped in Wapiti Valley on a bank of the Shoshone River near Cody, Wyoming. The wind blew from the south, so strong the walls of tent nearly collapsed. Inside was fine. But, we thought the whole tent might be taken as the wind whipped across the river. We ignored the weather and did not even bother to unpack the truck. Instead, we visited the Cody Historical Museum since it was open late, and saw a snapshot view of the colorful history and people of this area. A must see museum.

I went to bed as soon as we got back. A headache got the best of me. What I thought was going to be an ordinary night turned out to be much more.

I have never heard, or experienced, anything like the wind that night. Inside the tent, curled up in our cozy sleeping bags, we listened. At about 12:30 a.m. we awoke to sounds of destruction outside. Empty garbage cans rolled and pinged each time they hit a rock. We were sure papers were everywhere and trees had lost leaves and branches. As the wind gusts blew, the tent walls flapped, and it started to lift up and blow away – our little home had become unsecured. We found out the hard way that weather out here changes fast. Of course, we were terrified because we were still inside. When the storm finally ended we stumbled around in the dark trying to assess the damage. Everything seemed normal, just a bad storm.

Now it was over and we adjusted the tent then settled back in our sleeping bags and closed our eyes for the rest of the night. By now my headache had gone away and it was time to sleep.

June 13

The road from Cody to the east gate of Yellow-stone National Park is not only scenic but paved (a fact worth noting in this part of the country). Lining our way in the Shoshone National Forest were the massive pine trees and pleasant scenery. We stopped only to look at a rock formation, but this place is no Grand Canyon.

In Yellowstone, we camped at a campground called Fishing Bridge, elevation 7,792 feet above sea level. North of here is the cold water of Yellow-stone Lake. Our site is one of many lined up in a row. Visitors are asked to not feed the bears that wander into the campground.

The park ranger bellowed throughout the grounds. "Food that can't be put away promptly attracts grizzly bears, so be warned." A scary thought. I recoiled at his words, and we were going to stay here!

We quickly put up our tent and were off to see the sites. The thing to do is to explore. The park has a lot to offer such as incredible vistas, geysers and many hot springs. An added bonus is seeing all the wildlife. From a safe distance we saw a mother black bear lead her two cubs through a lush green valley, an elk who had spindly legs to support a tall body, and a female moose who sported a thick brown coat. Wow! Next, we found ourselves at Old Faithful, a popular geyser.

Old Faithful Geyser gushed and exploded, sending a pillar of water high into the sky—definitely something to witness. Nearby, the big Yellowstone Lodge looked regal despite its woodsy appearance. Now it is time to move on to other views of this spectacular park, so we went to Mammoth Hot Springs.

Mammoth Hot Springs are enjoyed by many. They are pools carved out of rock in a series because of terraces of different sizes, made from limestone buried over 600,000 years ago, and durable as well as soft and pliable. There are about

50 pools within the springs, and people who fall in never come out.

Mineral Hot Springs

We made use of all the turnouts and saw fantastic places. On the way back to our campground there were snowy, ragged mountains where the peaks penetrated the cloud-filled sky. Wide valleys rich with swaying grass crept up to the road. A variety of tall, fragrant trees guarded the park everywhere. Their ambiance is felt, and they seemed almost welcoming. The sun sank farther beneath the clouds and we finally, after many stops, got back to our camp site.

After dinner, our focus turned to bears.

"I made sure everything is put away," I said as my eyes quickly scanned the picnic table. "We should be ok," I continued, knowing our cook-stove, pots and pans, metal plates, and metal eating utensils were stored neatly in the truck.

"Let me take another look," Jeff said as he checked underneath the table.

"We don't want any furry visitors during the night."

"I'm tired so let's go to bed early," Jeff said. We were ready after having another packed day. It felt good to be in Yellowstone, but I fretted about what would happen at night.

I worried that we didn't clean up well enough and a bear might invade us tonight.

"If you hear something, wake me," Jeff said, sounding rather casual of the possibility of a nighttime intruder. "We will be fine," he said and went to sleep.

Campers in adjacent camping spots left scraps under their table. That night a bear couldn't resist the temptation and woke us by snorting and rattling. We quickly sat up in our sleeping bags. A bear was out there. Terror struck and we could not talk. A bear had invaded us in its quest for food. We feared it could get into everything in its search but apparently it found no food and sauntered off.

A dark green bear cage, positioned for use, rested on the ground nearby, if needed. Things were fine with us. We had received no bites, experienced no mauling, and our tent survived without being shredded. Crisis averted, we went back to sleep.

June 14 - 15

The rest of the night proved uneventful so we awoke to just another day in a beautiful park. Ho, hum more scenery and more animals, and Yellowstone did not disappoint. We ate our nourishing breakfast not knowing where or if we would have lunch but mindful bears could wander into camp.

We drove away ready for the day. Between Norris and Canyon, Wyoming (in the western part), we saw, in addition to tall trees, a mother bear and two cubs. They must have been tame because all three came up to the truck and pawed our closed windows. We were surprised and delighted. Our impression was that tourists fed them and they were probably looking for more handouts. We continued driving but not before seeing a female moose and her offspring, five deer, a couple elk and another moose which we figured was the same one we saw yesterday. A low-lying meadow heavy with lush grass and a creek added to the scene. At last, we got back in the truck.

When bedtime came I couldn't sleep.

"Having trouble drifting off?" I heard Jeff ask. I rubbed my eyes and before I could say more, he was deep in his sleeping bag, all settled in for the night.

"I just can't warm up," I said and massaged my legs in hopes that would help.

The temperature dropped to below freezing, we learned. The night before, the cold had frozen some water left in a cooking pan. Being from Minnesota, known for the cold, we didn't even think about it.

One night, Jeff got up and lit our white gas tent heater. I was sure we would die from asphyxiation. The tent had a rear window with a canvas flap, so we opened it for ventilation. By then, the entire tent had warmed. I slid into my sleeping bag and Jeff turned off the lantern.

We were going to hunker down for the night but I still couldn't sleep. I continued to worry about asphyxiation. Morning could not come soon enough and when the sun shone, I was relieved. We weren't going to die that night.

The last night was eventful enough and we left Yellowstone for The Grand Teton National Park, near Jackson Hole, Wyoming. We made our exit through the south gate where a park ranger greets visitors and takes admission fees, ignoring those leaving. These portals are more than ticket dispensaries. They are the gateways to fabulous scenery and fantastic wildlife.

June 16

Yellowstone became a fond memory, with its mountains, inviting valleys, and sharp-eyed animals. It is the neighbor of the Teton Mountain Range and the national park. The Grand Teton is the tallest in the range and soars 13,766 feet above sea level.

Jeff and I thought Teton National Park was prettier than Yellowstone, outshone Theodore Roosevelt, and surpassed in beauty any other places we'd seen so far.

Sightseeing is a large part of exploring the Tetons. We made many stops along the way as we headed to a campsite at the Signal Mountain Campground, overlooking Jackson Lake. We saw sparkling lakes, lush valleys, and majestic, tall trees everywhere. The regal yet rough-looking mountains acted like a backdrop to all these places. The Jackson Hole Highway was everything one imagines with its close-up scenery, regardless of each bend in the road or each pothole where we went bump. The Tetons are grand but there is more to do. We decided on two tours: The Snake River raft ride and a hike to places called Hidden Falls and Hidden Lake.

Running the Snake River in a rubber raft with other folks was great fun. The tour company offered half day or full day tours. We chose the half day excursion primarily because we had more to do that day. At the time, we didn't know the half day tour was the easier of the two; we found out later from the river guide. The thought of the upcoming ride on the river filled us with anticipation and excitement and soon we were at the river's edge.

We boarded the unexpectedly large raft for this 20-mile boat ride. Once everyone secured their lifejackets we began our four-hour journey down river. The guide rowed our raft as it wove its way through s-shaped channels in the river and its pass between mountain peaks. He told us a little bit about the area's geology, birds, wildlife and more about the park, all interesting, as were the people from all across the country.

The people on board added to this ride by re-acting to everything. They giggled whenever water splashed on them, nodded their heads whenever something was pointed out, and grabbed the sides of the raft during turbulence. Two people had come from Idaho, and two from Denver, Colorado, and two women sat near us holding onto the raft tightly and looking terrified. This ride was mild, but just by looking at them we thought they believed it was rough. They worked as system analysts for a small computer company in Kankakee, Illinois. In addition, there were two from Philadelphia, Pennsylvania, and from Grand Rapids, Michigan, was a harried father and seven of his ten children of various ages. Add to this group, one man from Cheyenne, Wyoming, one from New Jersey, and one from Brooklyn, New York. We all enjoyed the winding river, various animals, and fabulous scenery. Although we had to leave to get to our next activity, we took great memories of the Snake River raft ride with us.

Racing up to our departure area for Hidden Falls found us out of breath. We didn't want to leave the raft trip because it was fun. Now we were taking a five mile hike up a mountain to see a lake formed by glaciers thousands of years ago. A man assigned to us by the National Park Service was both our guide and narrator.

He wore a green uniform and broad band hat with obvious pride. Professors from universities across the country often lead these activities. He told us about the wildlife, plants, and how John D. Rockefeller donated the land to the federal govern-ment. We were there to learn what we could and to see things.

Were there things to see! A moose hiding in the bushes made Jeff jump in surprise; a small herd of deer ran in a valley; there were two blue herons out enjoying the day, a Canada goose teaching her goslings, we thought, and an osprey flew above us. There is a lot of wildlife in this park and we certainly got an eyeful that day.

We continued up the mountain to see Hidden Falls and Hidden Lake nearby. Our legs throbbed from the hike uphill, but seeing the Tetons up close was worth it. At Hidden Falls, our thirst meant ice cold mountain water would gush down our throats and bring relief. We cupped our hands around our mouths and squatted down to scoop-up and gulp the water.

Up at the falls, lava rocks hundreds of thousands years-old littered the landscape. Often, light attached to a water arc, and we were filled with anticipation for the explosion of color to come. At the bottom of Hidden Falls, the stream emptied into Hidden Lake, from there into a creek, and eventually, down the mountain where it dumped into the Snake River.

The lake looked like a picture in a magazine. That day the calm wind ensured smooth water. Tall pines that are always green surrounded the lake. We could have enjoyed the view all day the scenery was so great.

Although the waterfall was stunning and the lake picturesque, it was time to follow our knowledgeable guide down as it was getting late. But, these beautiful places contrasted with the rugged mountains of the entire park. Reluctant to leave, we trudged back on the same route we came up.

June 17

From Teton National Park we stopped in Jackson, Wyoming, then went up the backside of the Tetons on our way to Virginia City, Montana. In Jackson we saw a lot of development.

The city planners of Jackson wanted to turn it into a modern tourist town. So far, the village had a good start with its multiple restaurants, diverse galleries and unique shops. Just walking the streets and doing some window shopping is delightful. I believe they already are successful in their efforts. After we saw Jackson, we continued driving.

We stopped at a tourist spot called Teton Village. The parking lot was filled with tour buses, trucks, station-wagons, and cars of various makes and models. Shops lured visitors with a sampling of their products and services in the enticing windows. So, naturally, we went into one. After about 45 minutes, we came out carrying a plastic bag containing souvenir sweatshirts imprinted with the words Teton National Park. All the sites were be-hind the buildings so we headed in that direction.

Teton Village had erected a tram to attract vis-itors. The tram allowed close-up access to pano-ramic spots, normally inaccessible. In the snowy winter, skiers take advantage of the rugged moun-tains to test their skills. Many of the locals say the area is no place for beginners.

The hiking trails were well-marked and beauti-ful. The scenery here is unmatched, but we kept moving on. Idaho here we come. Idaho is narrow here and before long we were back in Montana looking at stands of trees on the shorter and less rugged mountains after stopping in Idaho.

"I'm hungry, let's stop," Jeff said. It was lunchtime and we pulled into the parking spots that outlined Little Miss Max's Cafe in Tetonia.

"What will you have?" The waitress leaned over our table. She was clad in her white uniform with a limp apron cinched tightly at her waist to hide her middle-aged figure, and she wore a princess-like tiara/cover on her head. She scribbled our or-der on her pad of paper.

While we waited for our food, we listened and looked. A group of men sat around a gray table drinking their coffee. We watched as eight burly men dressed in bib overalls let steam rise from their cups and heard:

"... got room for more potatoes?" one said

"I'll bring them next week sometime," someone replied.

Apparently, each farmer had underground bin storage for potatoes, and the storage facilities dot the landscape everywhere. We had wondered what they held and now we know.

The scenery made one almost fall in love. Everywhere we drove on our way to Montana, there were the rolling hills filled with farms, lined by short trees, in rows. Everything was green since it had recently rained. What a sight!

As Montana approached, we had driven through many small towns on our way to Virginia City. (We found out Nevada has a Virginia City, too.) One little town remains etched in our memories: Ennis, Montana. In Ennis, I learned about "self-serve" service stations. Until that time Jeff took care of filling the tank on the truck or a gas station attendant had the job. This time it was me.

"I really don't want to do this," I said as I pulled the hose and its nozzle from the pump. Jeff ignored me.

"Now put the nozzle into the gas tank outlet. Flip the lever on the pump, squeeze the lever inside the handle, and wait. Gas will then start flowing into the tank. That is easy enough." Jeff shouted this from the truck as I followed his instructions. After I filled the tank, my chest swelled and I tingled all over, I was so proud of myself.

I never thought I could. There is a first time for everything.

We spent the night in a motel in Virginia City, Montana. The motel was called the Virginia Terrace. Rain started and the wind blew from the north. From behind the tattered and worn striped curtains hanging on the window, we peeked out and watched the storm. Together, we breathed a sigh of relief, knowing we weren't out in this bad weather.

When morning came we had our breakfast and were ready for the day. A quick glance outside confirmed our suspicions: the storm was not so bad; there were branches strewn about and only a few puddles in the street. Overall, not much, all show and very little go. After a few interesting museums, we left this once booming, gold mining town for Butte, Montana.

On our way to Butte, a mining town similar to those we visited in Minnesota's iron range, we went through Nevada City, a small, ghost town leftover from the mining boom years. It has new construction modeled after old buildings. City leaders want to revive the town. It too, once thrived from gold mining. Again there was rain, so we did not stop.

The landscape reminded me of Minnesota only with mountains and more hills and valleys. I looked around and the area and I thought of home.

I envisioned my family out on a sunny day. Then I thought I recognized some friends. Just an illusion. Places they'd go. All without me. Suddenly, I was sad. What was I doing out here in this truck, going from place to place? Not knowing where I was going to sleep that night. Sadness took over my whole body.

"What's wrong?" Jeff asked as he turned his head toward me and away from the road. "Nothing," I responded as tears filled my eyes. Sure, Montana was beautiful, but I wanted to be done with this trip and go home. I had a bad case of homesickness, out here in Montana, at 65 miles per hour. Jeff pulled over, off the road, and rubbed my back then he tried to console me after guessing what was wrong.

"Things will be fine," he said, reaching into the glove compartment for a paper napkin to wipe away my tears. "Don't be so down, we have a long way to go and a lot to see. But I believe it's time for you to call your parents, just to check-in. You will feel better if you do." He was right and that night we hunted and found a pay phone. Then, after securing a campsite at some campground located in the foothills surrounding Butte, we drove into the town.

Butte is famous for its mining industry. Fortunately, there are exhibits to see so we could have a glimpse of the "olden days." Two things piqued our interest: the Berkeley open mine pit where coal was currently mined and the World Museum of Mining where we learned about the area's preserved, rich history of mining. We spent time visiting those sites and then moved up the road to Helena.

June 18 - 19

After arriving at Helena, the capital city of Montana, the local KOA was our stopping point for the night. We both needed a shower and our laundry needed doing so the KOA campground was the place. At night, we immersed ourselves in a movie. The next day was reserved for seeing Helena, but before we did, it being Sunday we went to mass at the cathedral.

"Look at all the tall pillars and stained glass," I marveled as I looked beyond the pews.

"This is impressive," Jeff replied "You wouldn't' expect a place like this out among all the cattle, it's too nice." He twisted his whole body to see the delicate statues, fine wood carvings, and the centerpiece altar. Truly a magnificent place!

The cathedral helped take care of the spiritual needs for thousands in the area. From there we walked to the nearby Montana Historical Museum, which was good. By now, we could discriminate between the good ones and the not so good.

The museum had three exhibits: one on the history of Montana, one on the Model T Ford, and one on the famous western artist and sculptor Charles M. Russell. Over time, we had grown fond of his art, so we had hoped to see a lot in this exhibit but were disappointed. Maybe we would have better luck in Great Falls.

Once we got to Great Falls, we found the Charles M. Russell Gallery and Studio. The place had some of his art but not a lot, so no luck there, either. We could size up a town pretty fast by now and knew we should move on. After a brief tour of the studio we pointed the truck toward Glacier National Park.

June 20

West Side of Glacier

Glacier National Park shares a border with picturesque Browning, Montana. It is cupped in the
hands of a valley of some rugged Rocky Mountains. In this small town on the Blackfeet Indian
Reservation, we looked for the Plains Indian Mu-

seum but instead found the Montana Wildlife Museum. Eventually, we located the Plains Indian Museum and a culture. Compared to the Cody Museum, this one had more artifacts. We learned more about the Blackfeet Nation and their history.

June 21

Since there was not much to see other than the museums, again we set our sights on Glacier. This is a place I've heard of but never seen. It was definitely worth the wait, regardless of how seasoned I felt by now.

Upon entering the park, we made our way to Avalanche Campground. The road was paved but rocky. In the distance we saw sheets of ice which we took for glaciers. At one point, we got out of the truck to look when the combined snow and ice that edged the road was, we estimated, over ten feet high. Apparently, as we heard later, the park service had opened the road to travelers only days before, and this was June.

We noted that the west side of the continental divide was warm. Fortunately, we camped on that side. Before we knew it, fishing and a nature tour were on tap. Anticipating, as anglers do, many big, beautiful but scaly and slimy fish, we grabbed our gear and found McDonald Lake. Our reels held line and bait used to catch our wet treasure. We baited our hooks, cast our lines, and heard our bait splash. Then we waited. After reeling in a few times, we decided fish would be nice, but we lost our line twice instead. For us, it was great to bask in the warm sun, feel the contours of the boulders we were on, and watch the fish jump. Even talking was far more enjoyable than our luck in the lake. So much for fishing.

But this was only the start of fishing for us. From now on we would stick to lakes and rivers in Minnesota for better luck. The next thing on our list was the nature tour.

"This tour is too crowded," I commented to Jeff as I looked at all the different sneakers and blue jeans.

"I sure hope we learn something," Jeff answered, adjusting his glasses before they slid down his nose too far.

A professor of Forestry from the University of Arkansas was our guide to Avalanche Lake. The tour was less interesting than the volunteer gave on our tour to Hidden Lake in Teton National Park, so we left the group and set out alone. For us, we wanted to see the area on foot, without the crowd. But, we had to get back to our tent for shelter quickly because the blue sky turned black, the clouds were no longer soothing as they turned big and ugly and rolled with the wind from west to east. Next came the lightening followed by the thunder. Raindrops started to fall and we ran for cover but there was nowhere safe.

"Hurry," Jeff called to me. By now, the raindrops were the size of buttons, and we tried to outrun them. Back in the tent, rain dripped into our eyes and we scoured our suitcases for dry clothes.

"That was so fun," I said as I wiped rain out of my eyes and off my face.

"We are absolutely drenched, and the rain is coming down in buckets," Jeff said, exasperated. "And it's pouring too hard to make hot chocolate."

In the tent we could hear the beat of the rain as it tapped hard on the tent roof. Jeff didn't want to brave the elements just for our cookstove, which sat in the rain on top of the picnic table.

"If this rain ever lets up," he said, "I'll make a mad dash and get it."

My mood changed to bleak. The rain dulled our view of this part of Idaho (we were now back in Idaho after leaving the area), its knolls and woodsy land.

"We've had our share of rain this trip," Jeff said. "Until now we have put up with it. Our patience has run its course. We've had enough."

"I don't know how we can avoid it," I answered.

"Just keep on moving," he said.

So we left on a cold and dreary day and made our way toward Spokane, Washington. We spent the night at a KOA in Coeur d'Alene, Idaho. Of course, it rained, and I don't think one ever gets used to it. Every day had some rain. No matter where we were or what we saw, it rained or had just rained leaving everything cold and wet.

On our way, the little town of Bonner's Ferry was of interest. Founded in 1860, gold prospectors on their way to Canada crossed the river there. Thus, the town was born. We were in a deluge of rain so did not stop. The thought of trying to dodge raindrops had no appeal. Maybe the rain will stop when we get to the state of Washington.

June 22

From Idaho, we drove into the eastern part of Washington, which looks a lot like eastern Montana with mountains all around and expansive, dry valleys, each with a creek running through it, compensating for the bleak surroundings. Starting at Bridgeport we saw apple orchards. This was June, thus blossoms on the trees had faded awhile back, now there was row after row of short, leafy trees in this barren land.

Interstate 90 took us through Spokane, the largest city we have been in for three weeks, and we worked our way to Grand Coulee Dam, the biggest cement structure in the world. A tour took us into the bowels of the enormous structure where, among other things, we saw the turbines that generate electricity. Afterward, we took our time to enjoy the nice day. Strolling the trails, we saw rugged mountains and pine trees everywhere. They grew right up to the tree line. This region is known for its magnificent scenery. But after seeing the dam and a little bit of Spokane we continued on to the central part of the area and Lake Chelan.

June 23

Lake Chelan is about 50 miles long and in the center of the state. Like most places out there, it is surrounded by conifers and mountains. Our stopping place was on the west end of the lake in a campground at the Lake Chelan State Park where we met Paul and Mona.

Paul and Mona camped next to us. She was about five feet six inches tall with long dark hair and eyes. He too, had long dark hair and eyes but was about five feet eleven. They came over to introduce themselves and size us up.

When morning came we awoke to – guess what – the sounds of rain striking the roof of our tent. I felt the comfortable warmth from my body and fought leaving the cozy sleeping bag, knowing I had to get up. I could have stayed there forever, but I got up and started to cook. With Paul and Mona coming for breakfast, there were things to do.

The rain stopped, and that made me happy. We were going to have dry guests. The way it had been, it could have been bad. But first I had to check the cookstove. Was it sitting securely on the end of picnic table? Was the white gas container attached properly to the stove? Did the gas flow to each of the two burners? All these things made the difference for having the smells of crisp bacon, where cracked eggs were made into omelets, and burned toast. When Paul and Mona showed up, the talk went from light to dead serious, but at least they were dry.

Paul asked Jeff how he liked President Richard Nixon. Jeff replied that Nixon was okay and refused to get into a political discussion with Paul. The truth was that we had no idea what was going on in politics. We were out here without newspapers and hadn't even see a TV news program. The rest of the world went on without us knowing anything at all. There was no way we could talk politics. As things unfolded we learned that Mona performed dance at theaters and Paul painted, as an artist. They came here from Seattle just as a break from their regular day-to-day lives. We understood their need to get away.

The conversation returned to lighter topics. Politics can be an emotional and personal subject. Everyone has their own opinion, a topic better left alone in a social setting. By now rolling our collars and sleeves were of no use as we braced for rain that tumbled down and wished Paul and Mona good luck in their adventures. We then rushed around packing all our goodies, dismantling our tent, making sure everything was in the truck and finally heading toward Everett, Washington, only fifteen miles north of where we camped.

Once we got to Everett we drove around and saw the sights. The rain never let up so driving around was the best we could do. We went to see the ferry pier in the beautiful Puget Sound. From there was on to the huge Boeing plant. Just the plant's size is the draw. It looked longer than a foot-ball field but had a rather plain exterior. The doors for the airplanes looked much like garage doors. A runway merged into a taxiway on the south end of the building with three 747's parked outside. This was something to see.

Next, we set our sights on the little town of Leavenworth, Washington, located near Everett and the mountains. The rain kept on coming, and on our way we squinted through the downpour to see some fantastic views. On one side were snowy mountains so we knew we were high. On the other we had steep drop-offs and a lot of rocks that led to wide valleys where sheep grazed. Wherever we looked, the area was a healthy green. No mountain passes or signs, just beautiful scenery. Leavenworth was just ahead.

The town wanted to be a destination area and they were working toward that end. Modeled after a German Bavarian village, Leavenworth sits serenely in a mountain valley, has a creek, and is famous as one of the top pear producers in the state. We also found the little town of Rocky Ridge. It had a fish ladder, but there was too much rain to stop, so our focus now was Vancouver, British Colombia.

June 24

We drove north and the scenery was still mountains and trees but now we got a look at the ocean. The water temperature had risen to the high 50s and low 60s ever enticing but we were on our way to Vancouver. As Canada got closer, we saw a few people approach the border. When our turn came, a uniformed, official-looking man came over to the truck, gave it a once-over and asked:

"What is your purpose in entering Canada?"

"Recreational," Jeff responded seriously.

"Where are you headed?"

"Vancouver, Sir." Jeff wanted to show respect for authority.

"Any produce, agricultural products or plants?"

"Only a few bananas and oranges, Sir."

"Hand them over, and be on your way."

We gave him our produce, and he waved us through; we were now in Canada. We drove through scenery that is fabulous, felt the wind blow at scenic areas, grasped at sturdy fixtures in the truck as we wheeled around each curve. This all felt good. It gave us hope that maybe we would get out of the rain in Vancouver.

The weather in Vancouver was ugly even though we escaped the rain by a few hours. Things appeared soggy with no sun to dry anything. Queen Elizabeth Park became our picnic place for lunch before we walked the streets and looked into the shop windows in the Robonstrassa and Chinatown areas. Still in Vancouver, we saw the Pacific National Exhibit Grounds before crossing a bridge to North Vancouver and British Properties. Just hearing words reinforced the fact that we were in a foreign country. Rather than stay longer here, we found another bridge and drove to Marine Drive in Stanley Park.

In Stanley Park we saw lawn bowling, an interesting and ancient sport. We watched from the sidelines as players, men dressed in white, took turns rolling the ball into a strategic position and tried to out maneuver their opponents. Their faces showed intensity as they grimaced and focused on each play.

"I don't understand," I said.

"This is complicated," Jeff replied as he observed the match.

We both shook our heads. This was a game unfamiliar to us, but we watched for over one hour, trying to understand what we were seeing and what seemed to have many rules.

"Let's find a place to stay tonight since we can't find a campground," Jeff said.

"Sounds good to me," I answered, needing to shower and wash my hair.

Unable to figure out lawn bowling, we left and settled into the Ramona Court Motel.

June 25 - 25

Lawn Bowling in Vancouver

Rays of sunshine poked through the gray clouds and we welcomed their warmth. Days had elapsed since people could bask in the sun's glow, worship its presence, or just enjoy a nice day. We hoped for a sunny drive to Point Robert, our ferry pier to Victoria. It rained instead. We loaded the truck into a garage-like area on the ferry where all the cars and trucks were lined up in rows. They stayed there the entire three hour voyage. The ship carved its way through the water during this time and we ate a fancy lunch in an elegant on board restaurant.

Our truck was settled in for the ride and we were comfortable knowing all our possessions were safe. Now, we climbed the ship's steps to the top deck. We expected to see a greasy, unshaven fry cook behind an opening resembling a window, but lunch turned out to be a surprise.

Looks of disbelief shot across our faces as we saw an elegant restaurant at top of the steps of this massive ferry. Cloth napkins, lots of eating utensils and stemware covered the white, draped tables. Smartly dressed waiters hovered around, ready to serve.

A waiter held the chair for me as and handed us menus to look at before we ordered. He then gave our requests to the kitchen staff and scurried to his position. After scanning the room I thought this was the most romantic place. My imagination took over, and I saw a cruise at sunset with a fabulous dinner, all we needed now were strolling minstrels and the evening would be complete. It's almost guaranteed to be romantic. Now, back to reality. But a blast from the ferry's horn jolted me back to this place and our life. Later, on the enclosed top deck, we found ourselves seated on red vinyl-like bench seats, and we started to talk.

For some reason, we were winding down. We both needed to perk up. So far, things had gone fine. The truck hummed along, the scenery was vibrant, the people interesting, and the experiences grand. I just couldn't put my finger on it. We had accomplished our goal of dropping out of corporate life for a while, so what was the problem? As it unfolded, Jeff felt a career change was necessary, but going from being a programmer to an attorney meant many evening classes and weekends devoted to studying. Was I up to the challenge? Of course. After we talked this through, we felt better, and our spirits lifted just as Swartz's Bay came into view. So it was down to the truck and back to camping. The KOA we picked this time was not up to the usual high standards we have had, but our sleep was important. Another campground was out of the question. Tomorrow we were going into Victoria in the morning to see what it's all about.

Victoria is on the southeast corner of Vancouver Island. It sits on top of some craggy hills, and has several things going for it: scenery, location, recreation, restaurants, and more. Victoria claims to have many museums. It is also the capital of British Colombia. We got a feel of the area and felt tourism was its future.

June 26

After we got back to the campground, the rain made us curl up in our sleeping bags and read. It rained not only at night but all day, too, but catching the ferry for Anaconda, Washington, was our primary concern. Just like the boat from Vancouver, this one was about the same size. The fine restaurant was gone, now a refreshment counter and rows of vinyl seats. A sweaty fry cook fried burgers and cooked fries. He wiped the wet out of his eyes with the back of his scarred hand. We would never eat there nor were we hungry. No romantic dinners on this barge. We wanted to be in the United States and this basic ride would get us there. Our crossing was uneventful. When we docked in Anaconda, a place for immigration didn't exist much less a line. Nor did we have to fill out any declaration forms or answer any questions. Quite loose. People, cars, and trucks exited the ferry and went on to their final destination.

When night came we stayed at the KOA outside of Seattle, a whole lot better than the one near Victoria and our resting place as we explored the city.

June 27

In the morning we were surprised by a sunny sky. Our spirits soared as constant rain had dragged us down. Taking advantage of our new found enthusiasm, we set off to explore the Emerald City.

Today, we saw the area from our truck which helped us get our bearings. We found Scenic #1 and followed it around and outside of Seattle. There is a lot to see in the city and it was a beautiful day. From Scenic #1 we wanted to hop on the Fun Run, a bus circulator which acquaints patrons with the place. We never found one so were out of luck. Using this type of transportation is a good way to familiarize oneself with a new area and decide on what to visit. Not to be discouraged, we found the Alaskan Way. It took us through the industrial part of town but we got to see Seattle's famous waterfront where we checked out some import shops before going back to downtown and the Space Needle.

At the Space Needle, we rode the elevator to the top where we found the observation deck. What a view! It took my breath away, and I'm not good with heights. Our breathing became deep in the thin air. I really think we had a case of nerves due to the height. Our stomachs swayed with the rhythm of the deck as it sashayed from side to side. At 605 feet above Seattle, we bent our heads and, from way up there, saw in a 360 degree expanse and from this great distance below us, the harbor, walking paths for touring, many buildings, museums and other places designed for the enjoyment of visitors. Seeing Mt. Rainier from here thrilled us. After eating we went down and strolled through Pioneer Square and Old Seattle.

Meandering the streets and browsing the shops is one way to get the flavor of an area. We did that before going back to the KOA for the night and visiting Mount Rainier the next day.

June 28

Mount Rainier is a national park. Standing at an elevation of 14,410 feet, it is an active volcano last erupting in 1863, and it has spawned six rivers. It is south of Seattle and Tacoma and less than 200 miles from Portland, Oregon. Because roads there are often blocked, one should call ahead to see what is open. Also, we found it less crowded during the week. When we visited, the fog had lifted and the sun came out. Oh, what a beautiful day. After all the rain, we were happy to have sunshine.

"The snow is pink," Jeff said. "I'm watching out for all these damn pine cones all over the road." He wheeled the truck as I shot my head forward to watch for them, knowing these large, innocent-looking tree remnants with pointed, sharp ends are big enough to shred tires. But these pine cones weren't about to impede our drive to see

Mount Rainier

what Mount Rainier had to offer travelers, such as the blue water of the Pacific Ocean in the distance, the Puget Sound, expansive overlooks, majestic peaks, glistening glaciers, old forests and more.

We had to secure a camping spot for the night so we kept moving. We were eager to see more, but Mt. Rainier itself was fantastic. By evening, we had pitched our tent among the tall, erect Douglas firs in the state park campground of Millersylvania

State Park, near Maytown, Washington, south of Olympia.

"Now that we're are settled for the night I'm looking forward to seeing Bremerton tomorrow," I said.

"Should be good. They've got some big history there."

"Can't wait," and my eyelids got heavy and began to close. I rolled over in my sleeping bag and went to sleep.

June 29

Battleship USS Missouri

The battleship U.S.S. Missouri, the Mighty Mo, is in mothballs in Bremerton, Washington, south of Seattle. We had to see it. The Japanese surrendered on this ship thus ending World War II. We felt very fortunate to see where the documents were signed, the mess hall, sleeping quarters, recreation areas, post office, and the massive engine room. The Mighty Mo is 887.2 feet long and displaces 45,000 tons. It was the last battleship the U. S. has built. On January 28, 1944, it was launched and after its many years of service it was decommissioned in 1955. Walking the steel gray decks where that terrible war ended made us feel like this was a holy place, and we were filled with reverence.

After experiencing the Mighty Mo we took a driving tour of the area. "Let's go see the Olympic National Park and its rainforest," Jeff said trying to fold the map, often an impossible task, while driving. We got lost out here, going down this narrow, tree-lined, paved but seldom used by the looks of it, road. We were on our way to Port Angeles, a small town abutting the Puget Sound near Olympic National Park. Eventually, we drove back to Bremerton and started over.

On this try, we found the Hood Canal Floating Bridge. It is a floating bridge that connected a few of the islands in the Puget Sound.

"This is a beautiful area," We are a long way from home but this definitely worth seeing. Look at the water; all shimmering and nice. Quick, over there, the white caps pop out of tranquil water now and again." I pointed to a fading wave. I also noticed the tree branches gently swaying in the breeze. "We are so lucky to be here."

"Luck had nothing to do with this," Jeff said, picking up on my comment I had just made. "We are here because we want to be." He gripped the steering wheel tighter. He braked as we came upon the Hood Canal Bridge.

The Hood Canal float bridge looked like most. All we cared was that it worked, and it did. We were close to Port Angeles and its visitor center. After resting there, we enjoyed the view of the grand Olympic Mountains and its serrated tops that seemed to cross the horizon forever. But I was bored with scenery; we had seen so much by now. The day was over and we were jubilant because a whole day had gone by with not a drop of rain. This was major. Also, we saw a small herd of deer, the first since Yellowstone.

That night, home for us was Heart of the Hills campground, south of Port Angeles. The place was near the mountains with an area suited for a tent. "I'll meet you back at the tent when you're done," Jeff said to me before we entered the rest room. I was never concerned about my safety regardless of where we went. So I headed in with my plastic bag containing all my personal gear.

I looked around the large room. On one side was a long row of white, porcelain sinks with bowls that sparkled. Mounted on the wall of each end were paper dispensers from which people cranked out portions of paper to use for wiping hands. On the other was a row of blue stalls. There was no paper or water on the floor, and through a doorway at the end were individual showers.

I selected a shower stall, entered, and made sure the door was closed. Then I stripped off my clothes, put on my beige flip flops, hung my towel, set the dial to HOT and, with great anticipation, waited. Next, I stretched my hand to test the water temperature and shifted my weight, anticipating what was coming. The water was still cold and, what seemed like twenty minutes later, I tried

again: still icy. I tried yet again with the same per-
plexing result. By now, my patience had run thin.
I wanted hot water! I quickly left the shower room,
threw on some clothes determined to get to the
bottom of this, then I spotted it. On the wall of my
little changing room was a small machine. Upon
inspection I discovered that I had to insert ten
cents for ten minutes of hot water. By now I was
angry. This is an outrage. Who pays for hot water?
It's almost a human right, and at such a vulnerable
time. Then I did something I have regretted; I com-
promised my urge to strike out and checked my
pockets for dimes.

After a hot shower and a good night's sleep,
we left Heart of the Hills campground and found
Olympic National Park and National Forest,
places we wanted to see before we left the area
and Washington. The only interesting parts are
the difference in topography between the eastern
and western mountains. The eastern ones were
not as tall or rugged as the western. We also saw
snow which made the mountains look like they are

right out of a picture postcard. But, we were ready for more.

It was the rainforest on the western portion of the mountains we found fascinating. Driving the truck was the way for us to see it. The rainforest borders the Pacific Ocean not far west of Seattle. Through it we went. To our left and right the vegetation was thick and all the plants were large. Each rock was glazed to the road with mud. All the way, water oozed from many brilliant waterfalls. Mountain curves added excitement to the ride. At times, we thought we would drive right over the edge.

"I'm scared, we need to get out of here," I said but the park was too beautiful to leave.

"We have a lot more to see," Jeff said as we rounded another hairpin turn. Then he began to list the sites:

"The ocean, where research is done, scenic views, the rivers, and the multiple natural environments, there is a whole lot here."

We found Mora in the Pacific Coast Olympic Park. After we set up camp we walked to Rialto

Beach, a public area. When we hiked down the shoreline, we picked up little beach treasures – small shells, branches that became driftwood, and a forgotten toy boat. Resting on the sand, we watched the fishing boats unload fish in La Push, another small town.

Then we retrieved the truck and drove over to 1st Beach. We spent time walking, sitting on some driftwood, and watching the water to help us relax. The wind always blew, but if one lies low enough, the sun feels warm. After walking down the beach and before a couple hours transpired, we sat on some driftwood and felt any cares we had slip away with the rhythm of the waves. Soon, a change occurred. Now, the wind came from the west, riling the ocean. Waves pounded the shore. Whitecaps rose and fell as if on cue, disappearing only to appear again. We didn't feel in danger of an upcoming storm or of getting wet because the sky remained blue. Tonight, we were going to a campfire, and it should be fun. The day was beautiful, no rain. One more day with no rain and it's a record.

June 30

Today, we took it easy. Most of the day was composed of routine maintenance. We ran into Port Angeles to pick up a few items since we had run low on bread, milk, jam, orange juice and the like. We found a market with creaky wooden floors that uttered their dislike of being used every time someone walked on them. A man behind the gleaming window of the display case in the butcher shop helped us select pork chops for tonight's supper. This market was the only place in this small town where we could replenish our supplies. The town had its requisite bar, cafe, gas station, barber shop and insurance office, no different than the many hundreds had seen on this trip. Only a comparison of its location could be made.

The town is here among these trees and mountains with water nearby. On the one hand, the view of the town makes a person want to live here. On the other, to get anything except the basics

means a car trip: think schools, clothes, and groceries. No real industry. Tourism is improving,
though, as people are beginning to come to this
small town by the water's edge. Close by are services and few restaurants. Our groceries were
snuggled into the truck bed, and the road in the
Olympic Mountains took us back to our
campground.

It was getting close to suppertime so we fired
up the cookstove and found our cast iron frying
pan. Our upcoming supper meant we were going
to eat those pork chops we bought today. They siz-
zled, browned, and we inhaled their smell. We
snarfed them up, cleaned up our campsite, and set
off on foot to the campfire.

That night we listened to a man who was a professor of geology at the local community college,
part of the University of Washington system. By
now, the sun was down. The day's heat lingered so
we wiped sweat from our faces and arms. Only a
few came as it was early yet.

In the center of a circle of straw
bales was a campfire.

"Let's select a place to sit not too close to the speaker," Jeff said.

"How about here?" I pointed to a straw bale.

"Looks good, now I'm ready." Jeff took a seat and awaited not only the attendees but the speaker, too. People arrived and found places to sit.

"Everyone found a spot," I said after looking around.

"Let's start, I'm getting impatient." Jeff got up, stretched, and immediately sat down again.

"It makes no difference to me. We have nothing to do and no place to be."

In came our speaker. His name is Paul, about 35, with dark hair and eyebrows, tall and oh-so-handsome. In the summer he worked for the Department of Natural Resources (DNR) and gave lectures at night.

"I think we are going to learn something," Jeff whispered to me, but his eyes were focused on the mountain in front of us and his whole body was positioned for an optimal view.

The straw bales became hard. After all, we sat on them for over one hour. Now it was time to go. We got back to our tent, inscribed our trip diary, and curled up in our sleeping bags.

ONE EXCELLENT ADVENTURE

July 1

We left the area on a driving day. Into the rainforest we went again. Even then, we were not im-
pressed. Perhaps we had seen too much scenery
already and needed change of pace. Well, we got
one.

Our destination was a place called Ocean City
in Washington. To get there, we traveled Highway
101 then turned onto Highway 109. Traversing pot-
holes and another scenic route, we enjoyed the
calm water of the blue Pacific Ocean before setting
up our tent in the National Forest of Ocean City.

The campground was perfect. Nestled into the
mountains, our space was functional as well as
beautiful. The fresh, mountain air filled our lungs as
we inhaled as deeply as we could. The ocean was
only a few miles away so we could smell the salt
air and see the ocean off in the distance. Jeff and
I almost jumped with delight over our good fortune,
but then we had a change of luck.

Each place we stopped required registration, just like a hotel. When Jeff went to register, he learned someone had already taken that spot before us, leaving us to explore because they had neglected to hang their "occupied" sign. He also found out there were no other spots anywhere. With shoulders hung low and a frown on his face he went to the truck.

"You mean we have to give up this beautiful space." I looked around at our tent, so homey among the tall, majestic Douglas firs, then with awe at the cloudless sky and the view of the ocean.

"Yes," Jeff growled, "we have to leave, so let's pack up and get out of here right away, I'll explain later."

In a rush we packed up all of our few belongings, tent included, stuffed them into the rear of the truck, and made a fast exit of the campsite and the forest. Kalso, Washington, just off of Interstate 5 a Motel 6 became our stopping point. A full day of driving made even cheap motels look good.

July 2

In the morning we hopped back on Interstate 5 and crossed into Oregon. Portland is as far as we would go. When we got there, we learned from the nearest Tourist Bureau Outlet, that it sat near the Columbia and Willamette rivers and is Oregon's largest city. Oregon is famous for many things but primarily for its rose gardens in Portland.

Before the rose gardens and after a late start, we found the Sorrowful Mother Catholic Church and hooked up with a group starting to tour the site. We found it a famous yet contemplative place.

When we got to the rose gardens, we were surprised to see the Rhododendron Test Garden; not only was it overgrown with people, the flowering stage had passed earlier in the spring. Bushes remained with only leaves and branches to see. Gone were the delicate blossoms. Now the soft, silky flowers of many different colors, from white to various shades of pink to purples had been re-placed by green, leafy bushes. Oh well, there is always next year.

We thought we would try again tomorrow since we were staying overnight in the Lewis and Clark State Park campground, east of the city. From what we could see only a few roses were blooming, but we enjoyed what was there. We saw what looked to be about four-foot canes holding large but only a few gorgeous roses. This was not the first time our anticipation fell flat and we left to do some shoe shopping at a big mall called Lloyd's Center before going back to our tent, showering and paying ten cents for ten minutes of hot water.

July 3

Morning awakened more than us. The green grass sparkled in the fresh morning rays from the sun. Birds of all kinds sat in tree branches while they heralded the arrival of the day. The geese practiced their fall migration, flying northward in v's in the sky, not knowing or caring about the beauty we saw. Trees with needles others with undeveloped leaves stood at attention. They acted as sentries as if helping to ensure, in their own way, that we would have a great day. The cold morning air filled our lungs and, although we were in a hurry to see everything, we enjoyed being there.

"I want to stroll the rose gardens again," I said to Jeff, "review the Science and Industry Museum exhibits, and walk in the Japanese Gardens.

"I want to see...." Now it was his turn.

Since we wanted to experience Portland and didn't want to waste time, we left. With the day was still young, it was off to the truck.

Out of Portland, we encountered Multnometh Falls and the Bonneville Dam. They were the places of interest. Before we continued, we took a look at the famous Mount Hood. In the distance was the memorable crown of the mountain. Wait until we see it up-close, I thought.

We had seen on some beautiful places on this adventure. Here we enjoyed long, deep valleys, craggy peaks, and the crown of spectacular Mt. Hood.

At the dam there was an observation area where we were able to watch Coho salmon finger-lings before their release into the wild. Salmon, sturgeon and steelhead trout all tried to scale the man-made, concrete ladder. Apparently, the people at the park had provided a vehicle to aid the fish in their journey up stream. This device helped us enjoy the site even more. After conquering the ladder, the fish jiggled and leaped to reach calmer water.

July 4

Some people celebrate the 4th of July with checkered table cloths and lots of family, food, parades, and grand fireworks to complete the star-spangled evening sky. We, however, spent the day in our truck looking for a campsite. No bratwurst, beer or even a campsite for us in Nahalmen's State Park. Since we had to look elsewhere for a place to stay, we headed toward the coast where we ran into fog and continued farther down the coast. Same story at all the coastal campgrounds we tried. Views of the water, sounds of crashing waves and the feel of sand were simply images until we got to Newport, Oregon, and South Coast Beach.

Before we got there we noticed we were low on milk, and I shut the lid on our big green cooler. It was just an ordinary cooler but it sustained life for us. In it there was a container of orange juice while partially frozen cans of concentrate floated in melting ice water. We had a half gallon of two percent milk, fruit, packages of partially frozen vegetables, a pound package of ground beef or whatever meat we were having at dinner, and to top it off, a loaf of smashed bread and a head of iceberg lettuce.

"Time to load up," Jeff said. "I'll look at the map. I know we'll find a grocery store somewhere out here."

"Let me check the other supplies," I answered, "and see what we need."

I walked over to the back of the truck, lifted the opening on the topper, and found the paper grocery bag containing our dry supplies, such as breakfast cereal, crackers and cans. "Looks like we could use a few things," I said, doing a quick, mental inventory.

Now we would go grocery shopping. After stopping at a small grocery store with squeaky, wood floors and big glass meat cases, lunchtime rolled around, even though by now it was later in the day. We found ourselves at a forlorn picnic table in Cape Lookout State Park, the weather still dismal. We looked at each other and decided we could do better down the road.

Late afternoon found us camped on the sand of South Beach State Park, outside of Newport, Oregon. About five o'clock we met our neighbor for the night, Ron. Handsome, with dark brown hair and matching eyes, he had a slim build and stood almost six feet. He was a Kent State student out seeing the country. We talked with him until midnight, about every conceivable topic from travel to politics. Our discussions were only that, nothing earth-shattering. They were interesting at best. About ten o'clock that night, we heard the booms and crackle of fireworks. Of course, it was the Fourth of July. We all got up and left the campsite, then looked up. All we could see and hear were the slap of the ocean waves on the shore, and the celebration above us. Everything was immersed in fog. That was our Fourth of July.

July 5

After some warm showers, we made a stop to change the oil. Maintenance was important and we always wanted to take good care of the truck.

Newport was a delight. Down at the wharf, crab fishing seemed to be dominant. Crab fishing is big there. Boats with stacks of traps lined the marina. Fishermen were easily spotted in their tall rubber boots and their flannel shirts. Their faces explained their lives. Deep facial lines told stories of rugged waters, harsh waves, too much sun and, occasional boat mishaps. We enjoyed the results of their labor by purchasing a crab meat cocktail from a street vendor as we strolled through the shops.

When we got back to the campsite we had a jolt. "Look, there's a note," Jeff pointed to something lying on top of one sleeping bag, laid out on the tent floor.

"I'll read it," he said as he scratched his head and picked up the piece of paper. "It's from Ron.

He had to go, seems he would like to hear from us." Jeff turned, put the note back on the sleeping bag, and then looked at me. "What do you think?

Without much thought, I said, "Even though we only knew Ron a short time it was a surprise he took off. At least he left us a note. We grew fond of him while he was with us. He sure liked to talk. We could drop him a postcard when we get back."

Sure, it would have been nice to have Ron around our campfire tonight, but he had his reasons for leaving, and soon it would be morning and our thoughts were on tomorrow.

July 6

Corvallis, Oregon, is east of Newport and far from the ocean with its main industries unknown. We didn't spend too much time there after a quick tour of Oregon State University where we learned the university is primarily a public research facility. Now we were on to Eugene.

When we got to Eugene the highlight was making a phone call to the home of a couple I knew from work. I don't know why I was so nervous, they are good people. As I dialed the number, my tension increased and I could feel my heart beating faster and faster, fearing the words wouldn't come out right and that maybe I was invading their privacy. The horror. Imagine my relief when I heard Tom's cool, calm, and collected voice. My heart returned to its normal syncopation and my worries went away. We had a nice chat and he invited us over. I declined because we wanted to get to Roseburg and Crater Lake. So with that Tom and I exchanged pleasantries and hung up. Now back to our comfortable truck and a look around before we left Eugene. The scenery was absolutely beautiful. Where else are there mountains and foliage like this? Interstate 5 came into view and we hopped on. Before long we came to Roseburg on our way to Crater Lake. We traded miles of paved roads for tall trees, green, wide valleys, mountain streams, and occasional waterfalls. By the time evening came, we were in a campground on Diamond Lake just outside of Crater Lake. After supper, we strolled down to the lake so we could appreciate it and what was left of the sunshine.

Scenic Oregon

To the touch, the water of the lake felt cold. Peering with necks bent, we sensed the lake depth to be endless. We also liked its shimmering clarity. A boulder at the edge served as a good place to sit and take in the natural beauty and tranquility. It was a good day.

July 7

Today was in stark contrast to yesterday. It started fine, we easily got to big, blue Crater Lake. It was just down the road from Diamond Lake, high in the Cascade Mountains in southwestern Oregon. Like Diamond Lake, Crater Lake was cold but clear. It is fed only by snow melt and rain so it's free of pollutants. It is said Crater Lake is the deepest lake in the world, about 1,949 feet, and is famous for its blue color. The lake is formed at the top part of an extinct volcano. It is surrounded by a wall of volcanic material. Crater Lake is considered an active volcano due to some activity in certain areas. After we stared at it for a while, it was time go to another site and continue this adventure.

So we left Crater Lake and its miles of fragrant, green, evergreen trees and headed for Medford. On the way, we encountered roads in dire need of repair. We had come so far, driven on different types of roads, but this was by far the worst. It remained so until we got back on Interstate 5 again to resume our trip. Then more adventure began to unfold:

"Take a look over there," Jeff said as he pointed to a campground outside of Medford.

"That's the best we can do," I answered. There, out in a field with no trees, no stream, or shade anywhere, we were going to pitch our tent for the night. But it got even worse. The restrooms were cramped and dirty, the toilets stained and unsanitary. There was no laundry room, only a single coin-operated washing machine and a broken dryer. That's not mentioning being out in a field where the wind was fierce enough to make even walking difficult. This place was unlike most campgrounds where nicer facilities and more desirable spaces were provided. "It's too bad this is the best this area has to offer," Jeff said. "We would have been better off in a motel. Maybe tonight we'll get some relief from the wind. Do you want to go to a slide show tonight? Someone who works here went to Hawaii and wants to show his slides."

ONE EXCELLENT ADVENTURE

What we really wanted to do was leave but we had unloaded our gear, set up our tent, and paid so we were there for the night. So much for Happy Hollow Campground.

July 8

After rising early, eager to leave, we took Highway 199 to the Oregon Coast National Monument, which is a series of caves in the northern Siskiyou Mountains. Northern California and its redwood forest were today's sites so we were pleasantly surprised to find the Oregon caves.

At the caves we took an hour tour, which was quite informative. The guide led the way over slippery rocks where we cautiously stepped. Down, down, down. There were eight on this tour. Before long we came face-to-face with tall stalagmites and the start of 15,000 feet of cave trails.

The caves were discovered in 1875 and soon became a tourist destination. Parts are closed off for scientific use but the rest is available to the public. The caves are truly works of art, sculpted by Mother Nature millions of years ago.

We identified Eureka, California, as our stop for the day. Although the caves were a sight to see,

ONE EXCELLENT ADVENTURE

we wanted to be in California and that meant driving. Perspiration dripped all over our bodies and it wasn't even noon. It was already a long day and it seemed much longer until we reached our destination. That night we were comfortably snuggled in our sleeping bags, showered, laundry done, and happy to be in California.

July 9

After Eureka, we put the memory of the caves behind us as well as the foamy waves of the big Pacific Ocean. This was Highway 101, a scenic and incredibly long highway. At one point, the famous Highway 1 meets Highway 101 and parallels the Pacific Ocean.

Driving Through a Giant Redwood

ONE EXCELLENT ADVENTURE

We stayed on 1(101) for a while, got off at Humboldt State Park and found Avenue of the Giants as we were looking for the Redwood Forest. Avenue of the Giants sets up visitors for the Redwood Forest. It's there we paid $1.00 to be able to say that, "We drove through a tree."

The Redwood Forest is just that. In every direction are the tall and old redwood trees. Park naturalists say some could be as much as 1,000 years old and can be hundreds feet high. At one time, there were over two million acres of these magnificent trees. That number has dwindled to just over 30,000 primarily due to disappointed folks of the Gold Rush who turned to lumbering.

We could have stayed in the campground of the majestic Redwood Forest, but, our goal for today was Napa Valley State Park, outside of St. Helena, California. Along the way, we stopped at an airport in nearby Calistoga and watched the gliders being towed down the runway before they soared upward in the thermals. The pilots of these flying

machines reported their joy in the complete si-
lence. We watched for a while, but we were starting
to think of tomorrow and what it would bring.

July 10

We had a good day. San Francisco was in our sights. Its unique personality coupled with its rolling hills had been the location of our honeymoon. We were eager to be there, knowing it had so much to offer. Now, though, we would check out this area.

Outside Napa Valley State Park campground there are miles and miles of fields containing rows and rows of grape vines. This is wine country. Mature vines are everywhere, three to four feet high with usable grapes at about one year. Vines are grown in any type of soil and in tidy rows which help prevent soil erosion. Grapes are harvested in the fall then made into wine and other beverages. We stumbled onto the Charles Krug vineyard and tasting room. Our knowledge of wine is marginal at best. Charles Krug is a premium wine; that much we knew. But we were there for the tour and what followed.

Several people took the tour. Conversation ceased as we all listened intently. The docent showed us where the grapes came into the winery, are crushed, filtered, bottled, corked, and finally sold. We left the processing area and cozied up to the wooden bar in the tasting room. Sharp-looking bartenders in their black vests and crisp white shirts took orders. Sauvignon Blanc, Zinfandel—both red and white. Then there are reds like merlot and port. Of course, we tried them all. It was well before supper, and the wine free. Simultaneously, we felt the warmth of the vino and the tingle in our heads as the bartender explained how to correctly store wine bottles, hold wine glasses, and sip. All this before trying the port, a heavy yet tasty wine.

Next up was the Christian Brothers' Winery. It looked like other wineries we had seen: large fields, sturdy out-buildings, processing facilities, and tasting rooms. However, it was overrun with visitors, all drawn to this famous place/name. The tour was similar to the one at Charles Krug. The real difference is in the grapes and the level of pro-motion. Hanging around was simply out-of-the-question because of the large crowd and we wanted to make it to San Francisco, so we had to get going.

Getting to San Francisco meant passing through Sausalito, the city on the bay side and the hills. It is in Marin County, well-known even outside of California. It is also a gateway to wine country. We pulled off the road, parked the truck, and looked at the shops. San Francisco and the red Golden Gate Bridge are just down the road.

San Francisco has a lot to see and we were ready for the cable cars, Fisherman's Wharf, and other places we'd visited on our honeymoon. Now it was the cable car that carried us to the Mission district where we took in the unique architecture and ambience of that part of the city. When it came time to go, we just jumped back onto the cable car.

The clang of bell, the rocking of the car, fighting for space to just stand, and even hanging on outside of the car as it braked and screeched its way to flat land were all part of the thrill. We rode it then had a late lunch at a restaurant we'd visited before.

In many ways we were trying to replicate earlier experiences. Now, let's do some shopping.

Browsing the import shop was fun. We saw goods from different areas of the world. We'd made several purchases during our previous visit so just looked at the offerings. With that, we hopped back on the cable car and returned to Ghirardelli Square, a cable car turning area.

"If we are going to get to Sacramento tonight we better move," Jeff said over the honking of the cars and the hustle and bustle of the area. Off to our home on wheels. Arms linked we ambled down the streets of San Francisco. "Look!" Jeff exclaimed. "Over there." He pointed toward an alley. We saw a man, mid-thirties beating up a gray haired man about sixty. This was happening in broad daylight. We looked around, no police to be seen. We quickly went around neighborhood again, no police. By the time we got back to where we first saw them fighting, they were gone. For us, this was a dilemma. We didn't know the circumstances of this altercation, feared our own bodily harm, and didn't know if the beating had already been reported to police. Back at the truck, we felt safe and talked about this experience. "What happened?" I said, still shaken. "Who knows, but nothing happened to us. Now let's focus on tonight."

The Golden Gate Bridge in rush hour traffic was congested and reminded me that living here, with all these people, would take adjustment. For now, though, the way north took us through more wine country. We decided to stay at Isleton, California, but ended up in Sacramento because when we got to the campground it was not only dark but it was flooded and no way could we stay there. We drove on to the Sacramento KOA and after our showers, settled in for the night.

Beth Grigsby

July 11-12

Today was going to be a warm one. California was having a heat wave. Eventually, the temperature reached a high of 110 degrees. By the time we left our campsite it was already in the 90's and the truck had no air conditioner. When we ordered the truck we thought we didn't need air conditioning. Little did we know. For us, the temperature was not important. Finding my friends Sandy and Bob was. Mather Air Force Base here we come. After getting onto the base we found their cute, little house. Sandy had been a roommate in college, and I had the honor of being in her wedding. Being there felt natural and so comfortable. We hugged and before I knew it, we were over at the modern-looking officers club reviewing the menu and chatting away like always. Bob was unable to join us because he was off somewhere flying airplanes for the Air Force.

ONE EXCELLENT ADVENTURE

Since it was so hot, we laid around and played with her dogs. She has two brown dachshunds who didn't know the meaning of "no." Before the heat got unbearable, we drove up to see Folsom Prison with its gray concrete walls and foreboding entrance through which thousands of convicted people have crossed. Folsom Prison was interesting and made famous by the huge country music star Johnny Cash. Of course, we didn't go in, but we wanted to see Folsom Prison.

July 13-15

We left Sacramento and Sandy at the Air Force base and drove to the Central Valley, a large supplier of the nation's produce, to Modesto. From there we kept going south through San Jose then north to Sunnyvale. Both were real nice, but many people live here. People love the weather in this area, but for us it was another uncomfortably hot day.

Sunnyvale is highly populated. There is no place to hide. People are attracted to the industry. Many hardware and software companies and others are found in the area. We maneuvered through the traffic trying to find our friends, Don and Janey, who have an apartment out here. A work transfer enabled their move. Since they both were from California it was an easy transition. They were truly "coming home."

We stayed with them for a few days. The first night we had the best Chinese takeout. Although they are gourmet cooks, it was far too hot to make anything. We spent most of the time at the pool, a good place to cool off.

One day, when we needed something to do, we played golf. The course was not at all inviting at 109 degrees. The amount of sweat on our backs was an indicator of how hot it was. When we returned, it was into the pool to cool off. While we played, Janey orchestrated our evening meal. Our feast in the cool of the night was roast beef cooked on a spit outside. Delicious.

The next day was Sunday and after mass we drove to San Jose. We had to select a wedding present for a couple we knew. This was going to be easy. There was a large shopping mall just off the freeway where we were sure we could find something. We strolled up and down the aisles, shop after shop. Nothing "spoke to us."

"This is the most frustrating experience," Jeff said, looking down the aisles of shops in the mall. "We should be able to find something. There's nothing here that 'grabs' me. But if we keep looking

we'll find a gift." Jeff was starting to sound concerned.

He was correct for it wasn't long before we settled on the right item. Because the happy couple
entertained others a lot, we felt they would use a
wine decanter and six matching glasses. So we
bought it. Now proud of our accomplishment, we
headed back.

With the gift beautifully wrapped, we left the
mall, only to get caught in traffic in the parking lot.
All we wanted was to get back on to the freeway
and go to Don and Janey's place. Exasperated
doesn't begin to describe how we felt waiting for
the traffic to move. Finally, we got onto 101 going
north when traffic stopped; this was Sunday when
traffic should be lighter. The frustration mounted as
we waited our turn. Our errand became an exer-
cise in patience, I thought, but then traffic started
to thin out and we arrived at Don and Janey's
home, gift in hand. For dinner they made a chicken
using specific directions found in a French recipe;
it was followed by a scrumptious chocolate soufflé.
I was hoping they would cook. We knew from past

dinners this would be great. We were not disappointed. What a way to end our stay with them.

By now, homesickness set in for Jeff and me. We called. Certainly, that helped. We had been on the road for a long time. We had seen so much, done so much. The sense of adventure had weakened. But there was more ahead. Were we up to it or we going to call it quits and go back to Minnesota? A dilemma for sure. It didn't take us too long to figure this out. We both wanted to continue. Most of time I loved being out here. Even though I got lonesome for home, tired of scenery, and wished for a real bed, this was the way to go. Decision made, it was time to leave the generous and warm hospitality of Don and Janey and head for the great unknown again.

July 17 - 19

We had not had a driving day for a long time. Actually, until today. Here we were, back on Highway 101 going south. We decided not to tackle Los Angeles. Both of us had been there before and would probably go again sometime. The thought of all that traffic and all those people discouraged us. Sunnyvale and the Bay Area gave us a glimpse of what it is like here to drive.

As we drove the freeway, the edges of the road, the median, and the grazing land were all brown. California's rainy season was during the winter and this was July. There would be no rain for a while. In the median were some drought-resistant freeway daisies surviving just fine because the plants' pink blossoms adorned the entire road system, and looked healthy. From 101 we took 46 then 99 to Bakersfield as we headed toward Las Vegas, which is not far from L. A., so people from

there and everywhere go to see entertainers per-
form, visit casinos, and stay in resorts. Everything
is available on the main street, or the Strip. The
neon lights, flashing signs, hordes of people, and
noise of Vegas contrasted to what we had just
crossed: the Mojave Desert.

The Mojave Desert is dry and arid. I am surprised anything survives here. Mile after mile, we'd
wipe the sweat from our foreheads, listen to the
wind as it thundered through our open windows,
and see water-like mirages on the highway. Finally,
down the road, we saw sprawling Las Vegas, out
there in the desert.

We checked into a motel at the end of the Strip.
Then we thought we'd try casinos. Not being gam-
blers, we thought we'd lose our money on slot machines. For being a pair of non-gamblers we sure
had fun. Just cranking that arm and bagging any
horizontal three-of-a-kind resulted in our cheers
and exaltations. Nickels and occasional dimes
clinked out of the machines and dropped into their
silver hands only for us to scoop up and count. We
lost a whopping $10.00.

We awoke happy to be there, despite the unending heat. This is a famous and beautiful place, and today is Jeff's birthday. We didn't have a party. There was no family around to help us celebrate. What I could only do was wish him Happy Birthday. We would make up for it next year.

We did do a couple things. Entertainment reservations were essential. We wanted to see a popular entertainer so we chose from a long list: Don Rickles, Phyllis Diller, Debbie Reynolds, Doc Severson, Sammy Davis, Jr., Dionne Warwick, Danny Thomas to name a few. More were there but they weren't on this roster. We made reservations for Dionne Warwick, dinner and the show for about $20.00 each. We hoped both would be good, but this night we had other plans.

Jeff saw an ad for a show in North Las Vegas; he wanted to see this show, so we would run up there to watch Trixie, Jane, and Cathy do their thing. Not being a star-studded show but still "riveting" according to the ad, we set out for this club. We went north on the Strip, past the hotels we'd heard of like Sands and Riviera. Then we kept going. In front of us were the bright lights of the Golden Nugget casino. This was North Las Vegas and was supposed to have better odds of winning. I don't know if that's ever been proven.

Once we arrived at the club, we discovered there was a two drink minimum just to get into this dark room with an empty front stage. Little round tables with matching chairs filled the empty space. We picked one, found a discarded matchbook and slipped it under a rocky chair leg. The show started in about fifteen minutes. While we waited it was interesting to look at the people: mostly men, which was a clue, poorly dressed, beer drinkers. I suddenly realized I didn't want to be there. Before long, the show started. Out from behind the curtain came three completely naked young women.

After a quick look, I choked on my drink and sprayed Jeff. I felt the heat of embarrassment from my neck up. This was not me. I wanted to leave. The women paraded around the stage, showing their naked selves without shame. As they began to strut, we left. I was so glad to be out of that club.

On the way back, we stopped at a casino and lost more money. It was fun to try. Every time we looked at the result of pulling the crank, we lost cash but occasionally we hit the jackpot and whooped and hollered no matter how small. When we got back to the room, the next day's agenda came up on the TV, including the weather forecast, and it was going to be another hot one. Right then it was 11:30 pm and 92 degrees. We heard sounds in the hallway of the ice machine valiantly trying to work.

"It's 8:00, time to wake up." I said as Jeff opened his eyes, rolled over, and stretched. "It's so cozy in here. I don't want to get up. "Listen," I commanded. "I want you to hear something. There's activity outside." We both crouched down next to the wall. Our ears pressed up to listen. Then Jeff got up, threw on a pair of torn jeans, and stormed out saying he was going to figure this out. He is a determined person. As he rounded the corner, he came to an abrupt halt at the ice machine. It was so hot, the machine could not make any ice. Instead of ice, water flowed into the holding area.

During each ice-making cycle, water would flow down, the machine would go clunk, and there would be no ice only water. In our room, we only heard the water. It had seemed we were in danger, but that turned out not to be the case. The temperature was too warm for the ice machine. Worry over.

After the ice machine crisis passed, we decided to drive and see the Hoover Dam. During a tour, we learned the dam was begun in 1931 and completed in 1936, Great Depression years. Its purposes are electric power, flood control, water retention, and recreation. It is 726 ft. high, 1244 ft. in length, and controls the huge Colorado River at this point. Hoover Dam belongs to the Federal Government, lies between Arizona and Nevada, contains the Colorado River, and cost 41 million dollars in 1931. It is also a thrill to experience. It is massive. Several people lost their lives when it was under construction. The tour and learning a little bit about electricity and the huge turbines used there was a fabulous excursion. But, we had to get back to Las Vegas because we had dinner and show reservations. Our truck felt like a blast furnace. This is the desert, remember. We had no choice but to endure. I tried to slide in my seat and I jumped around since sitting still was impossible. Everything was too hot to touch. Our hands re-coiled when gripping the steering wheel, to adjust the rear view mirror, or even to place something on the dashboard where we saw ribbons of heat throb and radiate. I don't know the actual temperature but it was hot! We had to go, we had to get ready for tonight and Dionne Warwick at the Riviera.

That night and over our baked chicken dinner, we met a couple from Pittsburgh, another from Jackson, Mississippi, and yet another from eastern Texas. They were our table mates and we enjoyed the companionship. We all expected a good show. Dionne Warwick came with rave reviews so we felt her show would be liked by all. After comedian Marty Brill warmed up the audience, he introduced our headliner. She took us through her hits and sang some numbers we never heard before. When she sang "Do You Know the Way to San Jose," the audience went wild. Everyone there knew that song. After a satisfying night, some of us went over to the lounge at the casino nearby and listened to comedian Louis Prima. He was funny, but we were winding down so some of his humor was wasted on us. Time to call it a night and head back to our motel. We were leaving tomorrow and needed our sleep.

July 20

On tap for today are Zion National Park and Bryce Canyon. Each is in Utah out in the wild southwest. Zion is picturesque from every direction. There are rock formations on surfaces high or low. Among the craggy cliffs and deep gorges, creeks carry cold water and a few trout. Bryce Canyon is much the same. What is striking is the predominance of the color red in the rock. Zion was established in 1919 as the first national park; Bryce Canyon as a national monument in 1928. Both experience rain only during November and December. They get incredibly cold at night and in the winter.

We didn't spend a lot of time in either place. The quickest thing for us to do was just to drive through and get a feel for them. We enjoyed the beauty and left to head northeast.

Bryce Canyon

We stopped at a KOA in Richfield, Utah, in the center of the state. Gone are the red rocks, the amazing rock formations, and scenic canyons. Now we had green grass, abundant water, and orderly towns. This area is in sharp contrast to the rugged landscapes of Zion and Bryce Canyon.

Beth Grigsby

July 21

Of course, we woke to the sound of raindrops pelting the tent, the first rain we had heard in three and a half weeks. Almost unbelievable. It was light but constant and did not impede our departure as we put Richfield, Utah, in our rearview mirror. Colorado was our destination so this became a driving day. Once we entered the state, we did make a quick stop at the Colorado National Monument, a series of canyons much like the ones in Zion and Bryce.

The Colorado National Monument was dedicated by President Taft in 1911. Its purpose is to preserve the landscape of the American West. John Otto, a contemporary of John Muir, a well-known outdoorsman, was instrumental in developing and preserving the area. Otto built trails so people could see ancient, red rock formations primarily made from sandstone. Desert bighorn sheep are found here along with rattlesnakes and other ani-mals. Songbirds and golden eagles soared and they found a thermal where they played. At first glance, Colorado National Monument may look like a remote desert environment, but it is a place with a long history, scenic landscapes, many animals, and more. We learned some things about this area before moving on.

After the Colorado National Monument, we drove to Montrose, Colorado and the Black Can-yon of the Gunnison. Naturally, it rained. Before we got rained on, we dodged raindrops to set up, then found a forlorn-looking yet covered picnic table in a public city park. It was there we ate supper hav-ing leftover deli sandwiches made with juicy roast beef and soft provolone cheese.

Our plan for the next day is the canyon.

July 22

Black Canyon of the Gunnison

"I've never seen anything like this," I exclaimed as Jeff and I looked at the deep Black Canyon of the Gunnison. This deep gorge is about 1800 feet deep, surpassing all others in the U.S. Some claim it is as much as 2700 feet deep. The colorful red of

Zion and Bryce was not here but the place is impressive.

The Gunnison River flows through the bottom of the gorge. I got sick to my stomach as I leaned out of a lookout and saw the distant ribbon of steam far below. Although the river looks serene, it is deceptive because it is cold, fast, and dangerous. It is millions of years old and is responsible for having created the old rocks, steep cliffs and craggy rock formations. The Black Canyon of the Gunnison is certainly spectacular, and we have seen a lot of country of many beautiful places on this adventure. But we had more to see. Now our next stop was Durango, Colorado.

There are no words to accurately describe the beauty of the Black Canyon of the Gunnison. But what was coming can easily be called beautiful.

In southwest Colorado we were surrounded by the San Juan Mountains, unlike any we had seen on this adventure. They are tall, some as high as 14,000 feet, majestic yet rugged looking, and red is the predominant color. These mountains are part of the Rocky range and are managed as a large section of the national forest and Uncompahgre programs.

At one time, mining was a big industry because this area was rich in minerals. Most of the mines are closed, but a few independent miners can still be found.

Mountains near Ouray

Our stomachs reminded us it was time to eat as we ventured toward Durango so we stopped in Ouray. The mountains here seemed fresh and alive. In the town there was activity and yet that small town feel. There are many places to rent a Jeep to drive into the backcountry. Full-day and half-day trips are available, with or without a guide.

After eating, we drove out of town to an 11,000 foot summit. We then pulled over and got out of the truck to look, stretch, breathe fresh mountain air, and take in the spectacular panorama. The view let us enjoy long, sweeping valleys, thick grass, and many trees. From where we stood, the Durango-Silverton (Silverton once a booming mining town) train puffed its way through a mountain valley with Durango its destination. Riding looked enjoyable and, perhaps, we, too, could experience it.

After bidding farewell to the picturesque town of Ouray, we were on our way. Seeing the Durango-Silverton train made us hurry to Durango. Once we checked in at their local KOA, we found the reservation office for the train only to learn they were sold out for the next three days. Our faces dropped, our heads hung down, and our shoulders slumped. We had gotten our hopes up only to be disappointed.

What we did instead turned out to be fun. After mass, we walked down to the train yard. Not only did we see train cars but we watched as workers turned the massive steam engine on the turntable. Now, after completing the turn, it was ready to haul passengers through scenic landscapes where they could have a up-close look at mountains, lakes, and valleys.

Durango-Silverton train

In the heart of Durango, there was a doll museum in which was a delightful visiting exhibit. I understood the lack of appeal for Jeff, so I went alone. The display certainly was informative. There were dolls from around the world, some new, some old, baby dolls all the way up to toddler size. One looked almost life-like with his blond hair sewn to his soft scalp and his plump, rosy cheeks. He was supposed to be a five year-old. For me, this was a break from unending scenery. When I finished it was still light, so we went back to the campground and setup.

July 23

Highway 160 took us out of Durango to Mesa Verde Cliff Dwellings. It's a short 35 mile drive. At first sight, we could only stare at these connected structures. This was worth scaling the long ladder from the ridge rim down to see the ancient ruins of the Pueblo People's dwellings from about the 12th to about the end of the 13th centuries.

"I wonder why people lived in these cavernous places," Jeff said as he looked at the vacant villages.

They were built using sandstone, wood, and mortar then painted a variety of colors, primarily beige. In certain areas there were hundreds of these buildings all built in alcoves or in and under a rock overhangs.

The sign read that they really don't know why people lived here. It speculated that the dwellings were closer to water than when they lived above, protection, or retreating from a great drought, who knows? They don't even know who actually lived here, maybe it was the Anasazi.

"The scientists and archeologists can only guess," I said assertively.

We then moved on. Our guide inside the Cliff Palace pointed out ancient discolorations on walls. Apparently, they were smoke stains made from fires built inside. We also learned that residents cultivated and planted corn on the mesa above.

After exploring Mesa Verde, the Cliff Palace, and taking some pictures, we once again scaled the ladder and headed back to Durango and our campsite. This was quite interesting but we'd had enough. Time to move on. Our eyes were heavy, we wanted to sleep, not drive. The next night our destination was a campground at O'Haleron Lake.

"Oh dear, another bad one," I said as I looked at this run-down campground. There were only a few campers to be seen. "I'm not staying here."

I believe I'd reached my limit. We spent the night in Salida, Colorado, in a much better campground where we reached a decision.

Mesa Verde

"Enough was enough. I'm so sick of all this." I threw up my hands in frustration. Jeff knew what was wrong.

"Do you want to hang it up?" he asked. "I know I do. My mom's birthday is in a couple days. We could swing by there and surprise her. She doesn't know we even thought about her birthday. It would be fun to see the look on her face."

"I'm fine with that. I have seen all the scenery I can see and we have put on 14,000 miles. It's time to go home. Back to St. Paul, family, friends, jobs, and everything we were used to. We set out to see the west and have our own experiences which we did. More importantly, we dropped out of corporate life for a while. Our goals were met and then some. We did what we wanted, now it's time to end it and go back. Besides, it will be fun to surprise your mother." I was hoping he wanted to go back.

There were a few more stops to make before going east to flat Indiana. Denver, the Mile High city, for example. Just recently, going to there would have been fun, but not today. This trip was over for us. We had accomplished our goals. So we took our memories of our time on the road and went home. We still had jobs, all we needed was a home, which was no problem.

July 24

Before Denver, we stopped in Leadville, a silver and gold boomtown in the late 1800's. Some people made and lost fortunes there. Leadville and nearby towns have rich histories. We noticed closed mine shafts dug in the sides of mountains. Leadville is interesting for mining people because mining is their heritage and played a huge role in developing this country. But, as part of our last hurrah, Denver held more interest.

The words Denver and Loveland Pass are nearly synonymous. The route to Denver through the Rocky Mountains means a ride through Loveland Pass. This famous pass contains a two-lane highway brimming with wildflowers and scenic overlooks. The traffic is as bad as any we found in California. If we had been ambitious, we might have forgotten about the traffic, thin air, and sharp mountain peaks and hiked some of the many mountain trails. This scenery is the best and eve-rything is green. The pass is on the Continental Di-vide and is 11,990 feet high. It is open regardless of the weather, and when the pass gets treacher-ous, chains are often employed, even required, by drivers to get through the snow and ice.

When we got to the outskirts of Denver, we got a terrible room at a motel, a place with paper thin walls and sticky carpeting. We cared, but not much because we were going home. Hurray, time to hang it up.

That night, we enjoyed a pizza from Momma Rosa's. We hadn't had a pizza in a long time. Melted mozzarella cheese covered thick red sauce, spicy Italian sausage, zesty pepperoni, and the entire pie was sprinkled with Parmesan cheese and Italian spices, all contained by a thin, crispy, whole wheat crust. Yum. I never thought I would get so excited over a pizza but here we were, en-joying this fresh, oven pizza in a ramshackle build-ing that had booths with torn upholstery.

The speedometer on the truck had broken. Un-fortunate, but minor. We never knew how fast or slow we were going as we made our way into Denver. A quick stop at the dealership turned into a half day event. The repair delayed us, so we decided to tour only the U. S. Mint. We could save the rest for another time. We knew we'd be back.

From the west we went east on U. S. 80 to Jeff's family in Indiana, the first time we had gone in that direction in a while. The flat land with row after row of green, tall corn gave way to little towns and one in particular named Columbia City, where Jeff grew up.

As we drove up the alley we saw his mother run out the back door, her light brown hair not betraying her sixty-plus years. She wiped her hands on her apron, and from her broad smile, we saw she was happy to see us.

"Happy birthday, Mom, thought we'd surprise you."

"Thank you very much. This is wonderful. You know how to make my day. Now let's sit out on the patio and tell me all about your trip."

After a week we had visited all the relatives, made small talk with the neighbors and store clerks, and wandered this little town while Jeff reminisced. It was time to go.

The journey home is one we would make for over forty years. It took us around Chicago, through Wisconsin Dells, and Eau Claire. We drove north on U.S. 94. Seeing familiar places was motivating. I could not stop grinning. It was good to be away but even better to be back. I thought of other things, practical stuff like family, work, finding and furnishing an apartment, and reconnecting with friends. The miles, even the rough ones, slipped away. Before we realized it, we were in St. Paul and ready to face our lives again.

Having this adventure was something we would never forget. Seeing many places and meeting other people were rich experiences never to be matched. Dropping out of corporate life allowed us time to reflect on ourselves, each other, and this big world we live in.

Our marriage survived being together 24 hours a day, seven days a week, day-in, day-out, through thick and thin. We looked to each other in hard times, and laughed together in others. It wasn't always easy, but when both are committed to the marriage good things happen.

We got back and resumed our lives. My mother welcomed us with hugs and kisses. It felt good. We unpacked the truck, knowing another camping trip in the near future was not going to happen.

Coming home with money in our pocket made us feel pretty good. When we left we had $1500.00. We figured we would spend about $500 a month. As it turned out, we did the whole thing for less than we budgeted, only $500.00. At the time gas for the truck was 29 cents a gallon, a room at a cheap motel was only $7.00 a night, and a good evening meal about $2.00. We were quite pleased. No one has to spend a lot to see what's out there.

Post Script

We returned on a Friday and Jeff was back to work on the following Monday. It took me another two weeks. I had things to do. Work would only get in the way and I was not ready to pick up where I left off. Our trip was over, now we needed a home.

Once we settled into my Mother's and Dad's home, we found that many apartments were available. Previously, we lived close to work, it made sense to again. Even the thought of a long commute was almost impossible to imagine. Now we narrowed the search and set out to find us a home.

"This is a great neighborhood," I exclaimed to Jeff as I explored the want ads. Listen to this: 'sunken living room, built in appliances, including dishwasher' and the list goes on. It could work for us."

Ads don't t tell the whole story and appearances aren't always accurate.

When I got to that apartment, the first thing I noticed was what seemed to be mounds of dog hair all over the living room floor. The entire unit, from the living room to the bedrooms was covered with it. The occupant of this apartment frantically vacuumed. A quick look at the view from the sliding glass doorway to the bare deck revealed an industrial building, compounding the dog hair issue. Certainly this place was not inviting nor did it suit our lifestyle but we finally found one that suited us just fine. It was a two bedroom apartment, in a nice part of town, and close to work. We also liked to have friends and family over, and this place facilitated that portion of our life.

Going back to Jeff's programming job and my office services position was a real adjustment. Our leaves of absence over, we had to put up with alarm clocks again, figure out what to wear, take care of grooming requirements, check the weather, and be out the door in time to be at our desks and working by 8:00 a.m. We were spoiled from being on the road with no clocks, no dress codes, few rules, and no schedules. We'd felt free.

When I finally got back to work, I enjoyed being there. Everyone I worked with was curious about our trip. On a wall, was a large map of the U.S.A. Using that map I showed them our route, told them some of our adventures and about some of the people we met.

At the time, I was doing a low-level forms administration job. During my absence the previous administrator substituted for me so everything was in order. That was a concern but one I hadn't thought about in months. I was updated on what was happening in the office. Now I had to reconnect with the people I knew who said it was courageous to take the trip. To some, living like we had seemed inviting and rugged; to others, downright crazy. But, it was something we had to do. We have always been glad we pitched that tent, enjoyed that view, and did what and when we wanted. Being on the road gives one a feeling of freedom. Now it was back to real life for us.

Beth Grigsby

Acknowledgements

Wikipedia; travel brochures; tour experience, Google Maps, and the members of the Madeira Beach and Five Towns, Florida, writing groups who provided the feedback so necessary. Especially Jon Michael Miller, my writing group leader, who graciously shared his knowledge and his encouragement. Thank you.